GARDENS *of* STYLE

GARDENS *of* STYLE

PRIVATE HIDEAWAYS OF THE
DESIGN WORLD

JANELLE McCULLOCH

RIZZOLI NEW YORK

New York · Paris · London · Milan

THIS BOOK IS FOR MY MOTHER,
JENNIFER WIEDERMANN.

AND ALL THOSE
WHO LOVE GARDENS,
GRAND OR SMALL.

Contents

Introduction

When the world's greatest flower show, the Chelsea Flower Show, opened its gates in 1998, one of the most anticipated gardens was Tom Stuart-Smith's design for the French fashion house of Chanel. Entitled Le Bosquet de Chanel, it was created in collaboration with Chanel's creative director Karl Lagerfeld, and designed to be a *cabinet de verdure*, a charming green room set within a formal French Baroque garden overlaid with a romantic planting scheme. The green-and-white palette, a symphony in simplicity, was a botanical poem to the spirit of Coco Chanel, who was the first fashion designer to make understatement look sophisticated. The white flowers included foxgloves, geraniums, hollyhocks, irises, viburnum, and of course, hundreds of white camellias, Chanel's favorite flower. The highlight was the central *parterre de broderie*, which appeared to be a delicate Baroque pattern but was the interlacing Cs of Coco Chanel's logo. It was a marriage of horticulture and Haute Couture, in one elegant, ephemeral stage set—the Chelsea Flower Show at its very best.

Fashion and flowers have always made for graceful collaborations. It's a natural partnership, a delightful kind of cross-pollination. Both are fleeting, dictated by the seasons, and can be profoundly beautiful. In fact, Mother Nature is such a glorious muse that many of the world's notable fashion designers, from Christian Dior to Oscar de la Renta and Dries Van Noten, have drawn on gardens and their beguiling botanicals to inspire and inform their creations and collections over the decades.

Some of the most famous collaborations between flowers, fashion, and design were those done by couturier Christian Dior, who had always loved gardens as much as women, fashion, fabrics, and gowns. Sentimental about his childhood garden in Normandy until the day he died, he drew on the memories and impressions of this seaside idyll for his fashion collections, transposing flowers such as roses, tulips, and lily of the valley onto his dresses, either with embroidery or prints. Even his silhouettes were often inspired by botanicals.

Following in his floral footsteps was Raf Simons, whose debut Haute Couture show for the House of Dior in 2012 was an extravaganza of florals that was designed as a magnificent tribute to Monsieur Dior. Simons orchestrated a glamorous stage set of flowers by decorating a stately Parisian *hôtel particulier* in a floor-to-ceiling tapestry of exquisite blooms—including orchids, mimosas, and delphiniums. He then sent models out in gowns embroidered with tiny petals, flowers, and fronds. One highlight was a dress covered in tiny organza blossom florets scattered over a full skirt, as though a breeze caused them to sprinkle over it as the model walked through a park. It was an homage to Christian Dior, and the fashion world adored it.

Lagerfeld has also designed catwalk backdrops using flowers and foliage. Mr. Lagerfeld thinks nothing of commissioning sets that resemble enormous gardens, and will often shift his shows to real gardens, such as Versailles, for full effect. For Chanel's January 2015 show, he chose the theme "Couture in Bloom," and opened it with four male gardeners carrying quilted watering cans to "water" the origami plants, which then opened up and "bloomed" into color. Next came models wearing lady-of-the-manor gardening hats bound with tulle. The show finished with a memorable finale in which a bride strode down the catwalk with four male-gardener bridesmaids in tow, each carrying a huge bouquet of flowers.

One of fashion designer Christian Lacroix's shows climaxed with a blizzard of carnations while the music swelled, creating a veritable shower of flowers. And Vivienne Westwood (herself a keen gardener) went so far as to dedicate her entire autumn/winter 2009 menswear collection to Andy Hulme (known as Andy the Gardener), whom she had befriended after they met outside a flower shop in Paris in 1994. Hulme, in turn, was touched (and probably amused) that Westwood would dedicate a fashion show to his unusual style, complete with knee pads, gardening gloves, and the odd trowel thrown in for full effect.

The Chanel garden, Le Bosquet de Chanel, at the Chelsea Flower Show in 1998, designed by Tom Stuart-Smith in collaboration with Karl Lagerfeld.

Above, top: The Nantucket garden of designer Gary McBournie and his husband Bill Richards. Above, bottom: The blue-and-white West Sussex dining room of designers Paolo Moschino and Philip Vergeylen.

Other designers and fashion houses, including Valentino, Dolce & Gabbana, Gucci, Giambattista Valli, Givenchy, and Manolo Blahnik have designed collections and catwalk shows that draw on the glories of botanicals. Valentino designed his exceptionally beautiful spring/summer 2013 couture collection to be reminiscent of a garden, with parterres scrolled over evening dresses, and the wrought-iron arabesques of park gates reimagined as evening cloaks and capes. The late Oscar de la Renta incorporated flowers into many of his collections, inspired by his idyllic gardens in Connecticut and the Dominican Republic.

In 2017, flowers seemed to be the prevailing motif in fashion. Some journalists dubbed the trend for florals and pretty things pastoral beauty while others argued that the new sartorial mood was more about all kinds of plants, and didn't differentiate between rural or urban, city balcony, or country idyll. Gucci's Alessandro Michele looked to the famous garden of Sissinghurst for his autumn/winter 2017 collection, embroidering roses and butterflies onto his fabrics and dresses and pairing them with glamorous wicker baskets. Dolce & Gabbana went all out on hydrangea-themed florals for their 2017–2018 collection, which they accessorized with wheelbarrows, watering cans, and chickens.

Behind the catwalk shows and collections, these same designers like to retreat to their own private *salon verts* to refresh their senses and restore their creativity. Some of the world's most impressive gardens belong to the fashion and design world, among them Le Château de Wideville (Valentino Garavani), Château du Jonchet (Hubert de Givenchy), and Ringenhof (Dries Van Noten). Van Noten and his partner, Patrick Vangheluwe, love their nineteenth-century neoclassical summer home and garden so much that they often spend weekends there making jam from the produce they grow. (Pierre Balmain was also known to sell his garden's harvest at the local green market.)

Other fashion folk are not immune to the pleasures of blooms and botany, either. Grace Coddington, Kate Moss, Philip Treacy, Amanda Harlech, Stella McCartney, Sam McKnight, Jasper Conran, Paul Smith, Hilary Alexander, and many others have all confessed at various stages that they love nothing more than retreating to the country on weekends to mess about in their Wellingtons potting, pruning, or visiting nurseries to browse the seed collections. (Kate Moss admitted to *Vogue* in 2015 that where once she and her friends used to talk about clubs, "now we talk about gardening.") At one stage, Karl Lagerfeld owned up to having a pair of Wellies, encouraged by his muse, Amanda Harlech. Celebrated milliner Philip Treacy spends most weekends in the garden of his Cotswold hideaway, where his beds of flowers often inspire his hats. "I love it there," Treacy once said. "I begin each weekend by going to the garden center." Valentino has also been known to leave his Italian headquarters to revive his creative spirit by tending to his flowers. "There are many things you have to do in life," he once said, "but you cannot ignore the roses!" Designer Jasper Conran also adores gardens and likes to go to his Dorset house most weekends. His previous property Ven House featured an orangery and walled garden; his new one, at Wardour Castle, promises to be just as beautiful.

The passion for gardens also affects architects and interior designers, who are influenced by nature's delicate and dramatic forms. Jeffrey Bilhuber, Peter Marino, Anouska Hempel, Axel Vervoordt, Bunny Williams, Paolo Moschino, Gary McBournie, Celerie Kemble, and David Hicks are just some of the designers who have made use of the fine lines of their gardens to inspire and inform their architecture and interiors. While David Hicks was renowned as a master of interior design, it was his garden at his family's Oxfordshire home, The Grove, which really showed his talent for design in his later years. It is still meticulously maintained under the watchful eye of his son, designer Ashley Hicks, and features geometric Hicksian lines, squares, and squares within squares.

New York designer Jeffrey Bilhuber loves to spend time at his Locust Valley, New York, home on weekends, puttering about in his tulip and vegetable beds, the colors of which are reflected in the rooms inside. Paolo Moschino and Philip Vergeylen's West Sussex home, meanwhile, is a graceful ode to the pale blues and greens of their garden and the English countryside beyond, while Gary McBournie and Bill Richards's island hideaway on Nantucket is an explosion of royal blue and tangerine, which not only happen to be the colors of their charming coastal oasis but also their favorite palette in interior design.

But perhaps one of the most striking examples of the beauty and style achieved by the cross-pollination of garden and interior is in the Dominican Republic, where New York designer Celerie Kemble has created an enclave of beach houses decorated around the theme of gardens. It is a fantastic folly, with foliage-shaped lights, palm-tree-shaped lanterns, ivy-strewn four-poster beds, and many other botanical-inspired delights.

The following pages take you behind the garden gates and into many of these intriguing spaces. Some designers, such as David Hicks and Christian Dior, have sadly passed on, leaving their estates as enduring legacies alongside their iconic designs. Others still tend their gardens with the same passion they apply to their projects and collections.

A final note: The gardens in this book are often the work and passion of several people, and sometimes an entire team. This presentation pays tribute to everyone. I very much hope you enjoy *Gardens of Style: Private Hideaways of the Design World* and that you, too, find inspiration in these enchanting places.

—JANELLE McCULLOCH

Opposite: White flowers fill pitchers on a table in Aerin Lauder's Hamptons garden. Above: Carolyne Roehm's Victorian greenhouse, which is often used for dinner parties. Following spread: The conservatory and view of the parterre garden at Bunny Williams and John Rosselli's Connecticut home.

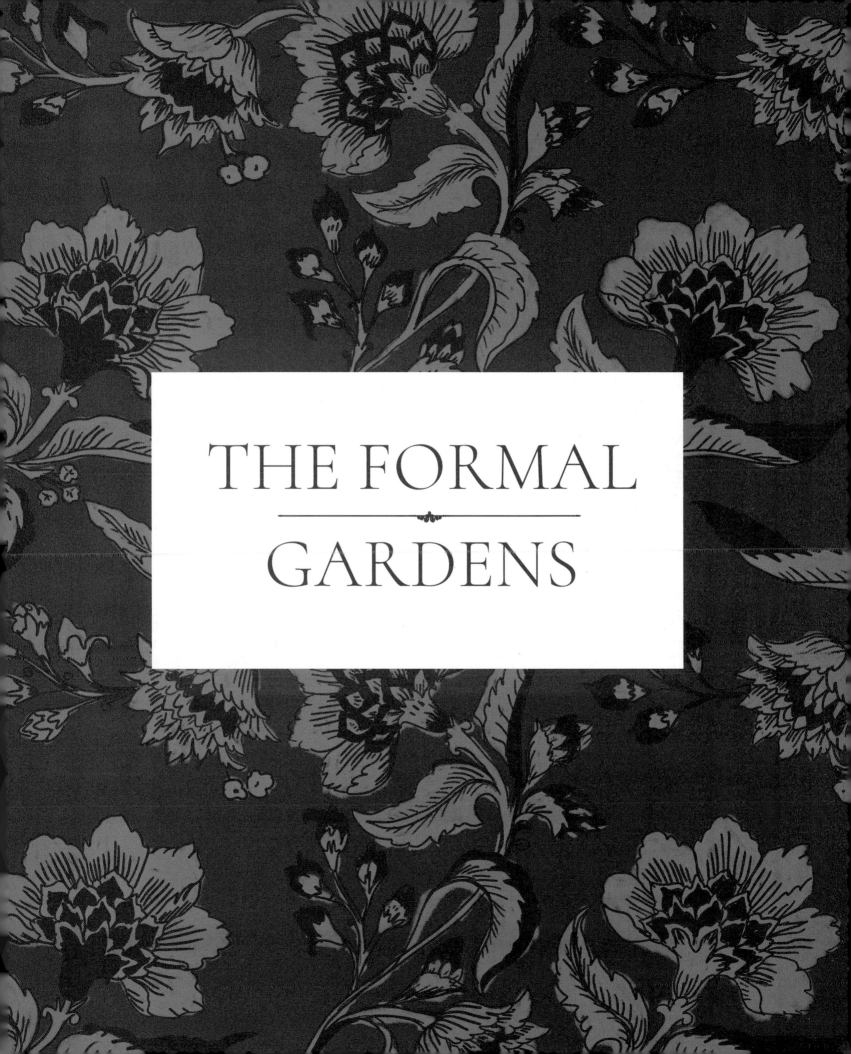

THE FORMAL
GARDENS

DAVID HICKS

Oxfordshire

David Hicks was famous for his work as an interior designer and decorator. His projects—usually identified by their strong lines, curious combinations (such as antiques with contemporary pieces), bold art, and unusual tablescapes—were so dramatic and so different from any other interiors that had gone before them that they immediately established his reputation in the international design arena. His clients and projects were wide-ranging, from Vidal Sassoon, Helena Rubinstein, the Duchess of Rutland, the Prince of Wales, and Mrs. Condé Nast, to the George V Hotel in Paris. He designed the interior of a luxury car and a pair of scarlet-heeled men's evening shoes—perhaps a forerunner to Christian Louboutin's now-famous ruby-soled shoes. Whether it was shoes or film sets, Hicks always delivered his signature theatricality and dynamic color sense. His work was striking, surprising, sometimes controversial, and always eye-catching,

all the while sitting on the right side of flashy. His designs have become so iconic that even now, several decades after he passed away, his interiors, furniture, textile designs, and paintings are all coveted as collectors items by the design crowd. They have proven to be timeless: classic motifs that stand on their own through ever-changing trends.

But while Hicks's interiors and textiles have been in the limelight over the past few decades, his garden and landscapes are where the real surprises are to be found. Hicks spent the last eighteen years of his life creating an extraordinary garden at his home, The Grove, in Oxfordshire. It was perhaps his greatest work, and he knew it: a place where he could retreat from the demands of clients, society, and life, to fashion a space that was truly his—a private domain and a world of his own.

Above: The Grove is an elegantly formal, all-green garden that reflects interior designer David Hicks's love of straight lines and geometric shapes. Opposite: Antique urns in the garden create focal points.

The garden at The Grove wasn't Hicks's first garden. He and his wife, Lady Pamela Hicks, and their family had first moved to an eighteenth-century Georgian manor house called Britwell House (named after the nearby village of Britwell Salome), which they bought shortly after their wedding in 1960. It was a suitably magnificent place for the designer to experiment with his interior design ideas and his outdoor spaces, and he adored it. When the house was sold in 1979, the family decided to simply move across the road, to a smaller but no less charming house on their estate. It was a chance to start afresh, to create a garden from scratch, and Hicks took on the task with enthusiasm. Though Hicks continued with his interior design projects, he was happier in the garden in his later years, and began working on *My Kind of Garden*, his last book before he died in 1998.

Inspired by the palatial gardens of France, including the potager at Château de Villandry, and by the work of John Fowler (of Colefax and Fowler), with his "wonderful hornbeam architecture" at the Hunting Lodge in Hampshire (now Nicholas "Nicky" Haslam's home), the designer decided to segment the garden into green rooms divided by hornbeam hedges, and to design each room as a separate garden. Each would stand on its own, like a separate set on a stage, but seen together, they would create a grand play: a "horticultural" narrative of line, form, light, and endless, memorable lines of sight. The unifying theme was the color green, but running alongside it as a dominant theme was the use of line. "I sometimes found myself becoming over-preoccupied with straight lines," he admitted in *My Kind of Garden*.

Hicks brought his design expertise to the landscape. He was a master of architecture, and The Grove is a sophisticated, architectural series of elegantly formal allées clipped into stilts, tunnels, and arbors. (Hicks was always concerned about verticals as well as horizontals, and believed there should be a balance between the two. He felt that too much of one or the other makes for monotony.)

Opposite: While the garden appears elegant in its simplicity, it is, in fact, complicated in its design. Visitors only realize this when they wander through, and come upon secret corners and enclosed hedged rooms that are hidden from the principal axes and allées. Above: As an interior designer, Hicks was skilled in scale, form, texture, and line, which are all evident in his garden.

While Hicks acknowledged that he was influenced by the great gardens of Villandry, Sissinghurst, and Hidcote, he decided to go one step further with The Grove. He incorporated long allées that lead the eye out through the garden to the fields beyond creating a harmonious link between the man-made landscape and the natural one. This was a deliberate technique to create vistas from flat land and views where none existed. Hicks also used stilt trees to disguise less appealing parts of The Grove's garden, such as the barn; indeed, standing before the trees you hardly notice a barn is there.

The principal allée is a long, wide lawn walk lined by pleached hornbeam—a symmetrical scene of grass and greenery. At the time of the garden's conception, Hicks considered planting chestnut or lime trees but then settled for hornbeam. These trees were the first to be planted in long avenues that stretched out to the surrounding countryside, to extend the line of sight from the house. Hicks was so determined to have strong lines (and long

vistas) in his garden that he bought many of the fields around The Grove in order to continue the elegant rows as far as they could go. Once the trees were established and then pleached, allowing their graceful trunks to show, a sculptural quality to the garden was achieved.

Soon, The Grove was surrounded by a vast tapestry of green threads, interwoven in a geometric, thoroughly modern manner. Even within the outdoor rooms, he continued his signature geometry, planting squares of boxwood within larger squares of boxwood so the garden was a play of shape: square upon square upon square. Once he had the structure of the garden in place, he set about filling in the interiors of those garden rooms.

One was designed as a pot garden, where giant pots had their bases cut out so the plants could gain nourishment directly from the ground. Another was conceived to be a secret garden, hidden behind old walls and accessed via a small drawbridge.

Above: The tower, built for Hicks on his sixtieth birthday, hides a secret garden located behind it. Opposite: Hicks was a master of the directed view. He believed in leading the eye through the garden to the landscape ahead. Hicks wanted people to look past the lines, beds, and borders to the views beyond.

Above: The ingenious pot garden, in which the bases of the planters have been removed to allow the roots to reach the nutrients of the soil. Opposite: One of Hicks's most famous textile designs is La Fiorentina, still produced by Lee Jofa — a geometric study of intersecting lines that echoes the parterre in front of the drawing room. Following spread: At the other end of the pot garden is the tower.

For the most part, The Grove's horticultural havens were fairly austere: unlike his interiors, Hicks preferred his garden rooms to be simple, like a series of sparsely furnished rooms. They were reminiscent of monastic gardens: simple, tranquil, reflective places to sit and contemplate life. He didn't want the distractions of flowers to detract from the peace and the views.

Eventually though, he acquiesced and allowed flowers, but only in a picking garden out of sight of the house's main rooms. Madame Isaac Pereire roses were allowed to grow over a wall hidden in the secret garden, alongside cottage flowers such as

poppies, pinks, and hollyhocks, safely out of view. Even the pots of tree peonies were hidden in "boxes" of English boxwood. For Hicks, this garden was all about the architectural forms of trees and hedges and the vistas they created of the English countryside in the distance, not the fleeting, ephemeral delights of perennials, here one day and gone the next. Hicks wanted people to look past the beds and borders, to the horizon beyond. He wanted a garden that stretched the imagination.

The Grove may seem like a simple design, but don't be deceived. Its striking lines are the key to its enduring sophistication.

Above and opposite: Although he called himself a gardener, Hicks was really more of a landscape architect. Like the legendary garden designer Russell Page, he was as adept at developing a garden's framework as he was in designing its planting schemes, usually around long views, hedged rooms, and other spaces. He had a great liking for trees, which he loved to pleach. Following spread: Another view of the landscaped layers of the pool garden.

Above: An architectural fragment forms a fanciful sculpture in a corner of the parterre garden. Opposite: Hicks always claimed he disliked flower gardens, but then in his book *My Kind of Garden*, he admitted that he loved roses, especially Mrs. Cholmondeley, Constance Spry, Madame Isaac Pereire, and Lord Louis, the latter named after his late father-in-law. "I long all year for the joy of June, when my secret garden explodes into a heady, scented paradise of roses," he wrote.

ROBERT COUTURIER & JEFFREY MORGAN

Connecticut

Gardens are often reflective of their owners. Rambling, romantic, double-bordered flower beds are loved by painters and poets. Highly structured gardens with defined lines of sight are often the domain of architects. And landscapes that feature gardens within gardens are often found in the residences of interior designers and decorators, who find it entirely natural to create rooms outside their homes as well as inside.

This is the case with Robert Couturier and Jeffrey Morgan, whose Connecticut property is an elegant extension of their personalities and professions. It, like its owners, is not only refined, restrained, and imbued with good taste, but also filled with humor. It is a garden of surprises, filled with strong architectural compositions. And the most unexpected element is that while the designers have shaped the landscape, their garden has influenced the interiors of the house.

Couturier is a French-born, internationally renowned interior designer whose projects include properties in England, Manhattan, and Mexico (where he worked on Sir James Goldsmith's residence, Cuixmala). His husband, Morgan, is a New England native and architectural historian specializing in early American buildings. It was Morgan who first found this idyllic site in Kent, in the northwest corner of Connecticut. He discovered a humble but charming eight-hundred-square-foot house, built in 1742, and spent three years restoring it. When Couturier first visited, he wasn't enamored with Morgan's fondness for austerity. So they built a guest cabin next door, linking the houses with a parterre garden. The duo loved the landscape so much that when two neighboring lots on North Spectacle Lake became available in 2000, they decided to build their dream home there, creating a beautiful, sixteen-acre estate.

Above: The strong, geometric lines of Robert Couturier and Jeffrey Morgan's garden echo those of the house. Opposite: The library is housed in an elegant pavilion in a corner of the garden. It features salvaged neoclassical columns from the Connecticut store R. T. Facts and is the perfect architectural framework to house the collection of design titles.

The five residences that now dot the property include the two original houses plus Dover House, a 1742 house that Morgan found in Dover Plains and saved before it was demolished, moving it to the entrance of the property, as well as a barn-style building, and, at the end of a long winding drive, the magnificent principal residence. This main house, built in 2002, appears grand from the approach—two pavilions with a small entry hall in the center—like an architectural hyphen linking the two sides. But the design is deceptive. Once inside, the interior becomes a charming, welcoming series of spaces ranging from large rooms to smaller salons, a deliberate shift in scale that adds drama as much as wonder. This property is all about the unexpected—Couturier designed it to be one delight after another. "I like going from room to room through small and narrow corridors," he says, adding that doing so creates an element of theater; one never knows what will come next.

Both men are passionate about decorative arts and antiques from centuries past. Couturier is a connoisseur of the decorative arts and architecture of eighteenth-century France, silverware, and Louis XIV armchairs. But he does not design spaces for show. On the contrary he believes that homes should be lived in and loved, as are all of the houses on this estate.

Like the house, the garden also feels easy to be in, despite its formality. The residence may only be a few decades old but its garden sits gently in the landscape, as if it has always been there. There is a delightful synchronicity between house and garden, between interior spaces and natural ones.

The garden is based on a classical design, inspired by the impressive formal gardens of Italy and France. There are several strong axes that act as a framework while offering long lines of sight and breathtaking views over two ornate *parterres de broderie*

and onto the countryside and water beyond. It is a predominantly green garden, embroidered with evergreen trees and shrubs with beautiful stonework throughout, from steps to ornamental urns and statues, which punctuate the space like horticultural exclamation marks. The different levels of perspective give interest to the garden as much as depth; there is the expectation that there will be something wonderful, something surprising around the next corner. But despite the European design, this is a garden that belongs firmly in Connecticut; the woods are omnipresent—there has been no effort to hide the naturalistic landscape here.

The main part of the garden is the double parterre, which is split by a central green passage of hedge that acts as an allée leading down to the house. It is designed to be seen from the house—parterres are always intended to be looked upon from an elevated height, so their intricate swirls and ornate forms can be appreciated. But these two parterres are also enclosed within their own green rooms, like delightful *cabinets de verdure* hidden within *bosquets* of tall beech leaf. The feeling of coming upon a *giardino segreto*—a secret garden—is further emphasized by the "doors" to each that have been carved out of the central hedged passage. The parterres may be seen from the house but from the garden level each becomes a kind of *hortus conclusus*—an enclosed "salon"—although the feeling of being within them is more akin to a *hortus contemplationis*, a serene monastery garden.

The various allées—including the two main axes—not only provide a framework for the garden but also lead the eye from the house up to the woods, tempting visitors to explore beyond the ordered borders of the formal garden to the wilderness beyond. It is embraced by the natural landscape, but it is also a conduit to it. Thus, wilderness and order become companions, two opposing aesthetics that sit comfortably beside each other.

The grand parterres caused great difficulties in the early stages of the garden's development. Couturier first hired landscape designer Miranda Brooks to design the layout and structure, but the plants died during a harsh Connecticut winter. A second landscape designer tried a new planting scheme, which failed, too. It was only when Couturier and Morgan hired a local landscape designer, who had worked on the nearby garden of Oscar and Annette de la Renta, that the garden flourished. The couple later commissioned designer Clive Lodge to refine the parterre so it would look beautiful all year.

There are several smaller gardens, including two topiary-and-lawn gardens between the parterres and the house, and an herb garden to the side, near the main kitchen. There is also an enchanting garden at the far end of the upper terrace, carved from a glade, where a circular hedge is outlined by tall trees. This place is so idyllic that you can almost imagine nymphs playing there. It is here, amongst the trees, where you can really see how much this garden has become a sublime Arcadian landscape, a true idyll. *Pairidaēza*. Paradise.

The philosopher Edmund Burke made a distinction between two different sensations, the "beautiful" and the "sublime." The beautiful, he said, was linked to the bound form, while the sublime was associated with the formless, the boundless. This garden and this place have both: the cultivated and created, and the wild and naturalistic. It is a place of harmony, clarity, and repose. Author Terry Comito, in 1935, said, "In a world from which divine and human law seems to have fled, it is only in such places as these [gardens] that the soul can recover its own poise."

Opposite: The circles and lines of the garden are reflective of many of the classical elements within the house. A "circle" garden has been planted at the far end of the upper terrace, in an enchanting glade where a round hedge outlined by tall trees has created a garden within a garden. Above: The collection of garden ornaments includes eighteenth-century English urns and a fourth-century Roman capital, all collected during travels.

Opposite and above: The garden is designed to be seen from the house as much as the house is designed to be seen from the garden, and nowhere is this more apparent than in the grand living room, or great room, where enormous windows frame the formal garden. "Gardens are designed to be enjoyed from the house," says Couturier. The green of the great room is also a gentle reminder of the color palette of the landscape outside.

Opposite: The square pavilion that houses the library has been cleverly designed to be octagonal on the inside, creating a more intimate space while allowing bookshelves for the couple's extensive collection of architecture, garden, and design books. Above: The white sitting room features a white settee and a daybed. The lake is visible from the windows, creating a connection between view and room. Following spread: The formal parterre garden.

NICOLE DE VÉSIAN (HERMÈS)

Hermès has produced some remarkable textile designers: Martin Margiela, Jean-Paul Gaultier, and Nicole de Vésian, among others. Vésian was one of the French fashion house's most talented designers, but she is better known for her garden design than her textiles and products. It was her garden, La Louve, in the village of Bonnieux, in Provence, that made her name. It still stands today as testament to her extraordinary talent.

Vésian lived her life surrounded by textiles and design. Through her advertising and design agency, which advised clients on textiles and trends, she had built up an international reputation as a fabric specialist, traveling between New York and Paris every month. Then, in 1976, Hermès called, and so, and at the age of sixty, she went to work for the venerated French company in Paris as the director of the lifestyle collections. She designed

clothing, tableware, gardening tools, and even yacht interiors and Renault cars. In 1985, at the age of sixty-nine, she decided to retire. But the creative urge hadn't left her. What could she do? What could she take on that she had enough energy for, and that didn't take a great deal of money? Then she fell in love—with a garden in Provence.

Provence is like a giant textile spread over the South of France; a weave of fields, vineyards, orchards, woodlands, wild ravines, cliffs, gentle country lanes, and quiet rural villages. Here, as in the world of textiles and fashion, the panoramas of patterns, textures, and colors change from season to season. Vésian found this landscape comforting. So, when she decided to leave Paris on the approach of her seventieth birthday, she headed south to set up a new life, at a rundown garden in a remote village. A garden called La Louve.

Above and opposite: Designed by Nicole de Vésian, the former director of the lifestyle collections at Hermès, the all-green Mediterranean garden of La Louve in Provence is a sublime tapestry of patterns, forms, textures, and lines composed to look like the weave of fabric.

La Louve (French for "She-Wolf") appealed to this designer searching for a new project at a late stage of life. The property was clearly derelict and badly in need of repairs, but there was something romantic about the site. She bought it and began work.

Vésian wasn't new to gardening. She had grown food for her family during World War II and tended to small gardens in Paris. But La Louve was on a whole other level. It was probably the most difficult garden she could have chosen; the weather, the site, and the difficulties of getting materials up and down the steep slope all added issues to an already challenging property. But Vésian was no lightweight. And she wasn't silly. Applying her practicality, resourcefulness, and frugality, she asked local nurserymen to save their ailing and unsalable plants, which she then brought home and nursed back to life. She collected plants, river stones, and rocks from the landscape to create natural plantings, no-expense stone walls, and steps. "I always avoid extravagance and expense," she said. But she also knew her limits: she hired tradesmen and masons to move the heavy stone, but also worked alongside them to ensure they set the right stones down in the right places, on pathways, in retaining walls, and on garden-bed edges. She wanted it to look like the ruined walls of the village. When one stonemason arranged the stones in a perfect line, she made him rearrange them so there was looseness to the line. The hillside stone and the local plants worked beautifully together to create a garden that was at home in its setting. Vésian wanted the garden to look as though it had always been there, and it did. It was a harmonious balance of natural and man-made. As British writer and garden designer Tania Compton said, the garden was an "homage" to the hills of Provence.

Even the way Vésian pruned her plants was done to create a natural look; one would be softly clipped and another would be left to grow unchecked. "Nature shaped the plants; I just help them along," she told Louisa Jones, her friend and biographer, who chronicled the development of the garden in her best-selling book *Nicole de Vésian: Gardens, Modern Design in Provence*. It was a garden that felt fluid, rather than stilted and over-clipped. She hated symmetry. Neat, straight, organized lines had no place here.

What Vésian was doing was creating a "textile" garden, one that was designed to be seen from above, looking down from the upper terrace. "I am so attached to textiles. Very few people *feel* gardens," she told the writer Mirabel Osler. The site tumbled down a hillside over several, very steep levels, with the top terrace being the site of the house, the middle levels being the main garden, and the lower level featuring a lavender parterre. As the eye followed these levels down and out over the lavender and across the countryside to the vineyards and mountains beyond, people felt as though the garden was at one with the landscape. It was intended to be an intricate interplay of leaf and layers, especially in late afternoon when the sun dipped below the hills and sent light and shadows across the boxwood, rosemary, and laurustinus.

As a designer, Vésian was very aware of the subtle variations of patterns, lines, proportions, colors, and texture, and the way they harmonized with or were juxtaposed against each other. Her mastery of foliage was as great as her mastery of fabric. As a result, La Louve is an embroidery of the most beautiful kind—the sublime creation of a master of textiles meeting the

Opposite and this page: The gardens are laid out on a series of terraces, and are designed to be in harmony with the surrounding mountainous terrain. The paths, edges, and beds incorporate local rocks and stones, including those from the nearby river, an approach that integrates the garden further with the local landscape. Trees and bushes are trimmed into geometric shapes, and while the garden has mostly green foliage-based plants, there are some flowers, including roses and irises, and native fragrant plants of the region, including lavender, rosemary, and santolina. Following spread: The lavender parterre on the lower terrace.

natural world. And it's no wonder it influenced not just other gardeners but also many designers.

It was no surprise that La Louve launched a new career for Vésian. As a result she was asked to design gardens for many people, including filmmaker Ridley Scott. She spent just over a decade at La Louve, before selling it in 1996 to move on to a smaller garden. (She died before she could fully restore her next garden.) But La Louve went on to be owned by two other gardeners, who adored Vésian's work and happily opened it up to small groups of visitors each year. The first was art collector Judith Pillsbury, who preserved the original design and maintained the garden until 2014 before selling it to present owner Sylvie Verger-Lanel, who has made small changes that respect the original design.

There's an old saying: When a gardener dies, the garden often does, too. Thankfully, in this instance, that's far from true. You only have to wander the paths at sunset to feel that Vésian is still there, clipping her topiary and looking out onto her beloved Provence landscape.

The mountainous landscape of Bonnieux, the village in which La Louve is located. The garden is hidden on this steep slope, behind the village, where it looks out to the Provence hills. It has been classified by the French Ministry of Culture as one of the Notable Gardens of France.

PAOLO MOSCHINO & PHILIP VERGEYLEN

West Sussex

Most people in the international design world know of Nicholas "Nicky" Haslam, the legendary British designer and flamboyant gentleman-about-town. In the 1980s, Nicholas and his partner, in both business and life, Paolo Moschino, ran one of the top interior design businesses in London. Many of their employees, including Cath Kidston, went on to high-profile businesses of their own.

But then the pair decided to (amicably) divide the business in 1995, with Haslam taking control of NH Design and Moschino taking ownership of the Nicholas Haslam store, which creates and sells furniture, fabrics, and lighting, as well as antiques. Twenty years on, Haslam is still a highly regarded design name, while Moschino has achieved his own fame. Moschino is the still-successful proprietor of the Nicholas Haslam store in Pimlico in London, and the design studio that has evolved

from it, but he has also become the interior designer of choice for, as one fan puts it, "the inconspicuous rich"—those who like their interior spaces to be as discreet as their financial advisors. Spend a few minutes with Italian-born Moschino and his partner, Belgium-born Philip Vergeylen, and you can see why their clients adore them. If they weren't interior designers, they'd make first-class diplomats.

Moschino and Vergeylen spend most of the week in London, when they're not traveling abroad to oversee projects and meet with clients, but Friday nights they head to West Sussex, where a sublime country house has become their principal residence. When they first saw it, they fell in love with it on the spot: the location and architecture alone were enough to persuade them that it was a good buy, even before they walked inside. But the couple had their work cut out for them.

Above: Paolo Moschino and Philip Vergeylen's garden is a serene, elegantly proportioned space of green rooms that flow into one another. Opposite: A dapper stone statue is dressed in ivy.

The exterior was a charming mix of Tudor and nineteenth-century style, set in large grounds with a matching barn, which has since been converted to extensive guest quarters. However, the interior of the main residence was a labyrinth of poky, dim rooms set around a huge Tudor chimney, and it's difficult to imagine how they reconfigured it into a series of light, white, elegant spaces without pulling the whole house apart and starting again. Certain parts were edited: an ugly rear extension was removed, and walls of other rooms were taken down to create larger spaces that flow easily into each other. Other parts, considered too beautiful to remove, were retained, including many of the original beamed ceilings and wide wooden floors.

Now, the house has a new life—and a new atmosphere. The undisputed heart of the home is the all-white kitchen, a conservatory-style space that looks over a gathering of neat topiary trees in different-sized terra-cotta tubs and then on to a sweep of manicured English lawn to fields beyond. Next to this is a stunning blue-and-white dining room, which has achieved a level of fame of its own for the hand-painted blue-and-white mural by Dawn Reader on the wall. Farther along are a double drawing room and cozy sitting room, and upstairs are well-appointed bedrooms that overlook the parterre garden. The main color palette is pale blue, white, and a chalky cream shade, with splashes of chocolate and green. The furniture is either pale or painted wood.

But while it all seems subdued and understated, this is not an interior that is boring. These gentlemen may trade in sophistication and their currency may be elegance of the highest order, but they are also very fond of wit and humor—in both their conversations and in their living spaces. Rooms are studies in style but many of the spaces are also entertaining. For example, a sweet little powder room covered with bamboo prints includes a mini library of books to read, while the Bloody Mary–red sitting room—an anomaly in the otherwise blue-hued house—is a wink to color and creativity.

Above: The dominant palette of the house's interior is white, off-white, and pale blue, creating a sense of serenity. Opposite: Clipped boxwood forms a collection of delightful topiary on the terrace, the couple's favorite place to sit and read.

Opposite: The airy, bright, white kitchen has been fashioned like a conservatory, with picture windows that frame the garden and French doors to the terrace. Above: The rear terrace is the couple's favorite place to dine in the summer months. Left: The lettuceware and the cabbageware create a lovely connection between the garden and entertaining.

The blue-and-white dining room and its famous blue-and-white painted mural is one of the best-known dining rooms in the interior design world. The hand-painted mural, by artist Dawn Reader, is based on both their collection of blue-and-white Delft porcelain and the eighteenth-century painted French screen that hangs on the wall.

Above: The bed in the guest bedroom is nineteenth-century French. The wall murals have been painted freehand by well-known artist Dawn Reader in a garden-inspired design that reflects the colors of the Le Manach fabric of the bedcover and curtains. Opposite: In the entrance hall, a seventeenth-century Flemish tapestry, a pair of Belgian lamps made from cast-iron balusters, and a terra-cotta bust of Madame du Barry, Louis XV's last mistress, make a charming tableau.

It's outside where the real drama is to be found. Moschino and Vergeylen may be in-demand designers during the week, but they are quiet country gardeners on weekends—and happily show their fingernails to prove it. These are two men who would rather dig up the weeds themselves than employ someone to do it, and that says a lot about their grounded nature and unpretentious style. But—like all interior designers who venture out into the garden—these two find it difficult to leave their unerring eye for fine lines and pleasing forms at the French doors of their sitting and dining rooms and the kitchen. Pots of English boxwood have been clipped into "clouds" and positioned in chic groupings, while antique urns have been planted with fast-growing ivy and placed between elegantly pleached trees. A formal parterre forms a stylish entrance to the front of the house, and even the guest cottage has its own Elizabeth knot garden to gaze out upon.

Elsewhere, the side lawn—mowed in stripes of near mathematical precision—unfurls down past a bed of palest pink roses and dahlias on one side and a series of spout fountains on the other to end in a formal display of antique urns. And the pool area features stylish deckchairs set between blue-and-white porcelain stools.

It is a far different picture to how it looked when they first arrived. "When we bought the property, there was land around the house but no garden. And to begin with, we found it challenging, particularly when it came to designing without boundaries, as I am used to having walls!" says Vergeylen. "For both of us, everything finally fell into place when we decided our garden should have rooms." They began treating it as they would a house, planning

and creating spaces so that each green room felt like a welcoming, intriguing place to wander into and linger for a little while. Eventually the garden and its enormous, boundary-less expanse was broken up into enclosures, bordered by hedges and beds, although the rear was left without walls to retain the view to the fields. Now there is a series of harmonious, well-proportioned mini-gardens, including a long garden, a pool garden, a front parterre, a terrace, and a woodland corner, where a bench of "twigs" made from concrete *faux bois* invites visitors to sit.

The couple says their favorite place to relax is on the sunny terrace just outside the sitting room, which is layered with green clouds of boxwood, inspired by the landscape designs of Jacques Wirtz. They also say that while the garden is a mostly formal green affair, they have been seduced by color—particularly when it comes to dahlias. Several borders are planted with the huge flowers, which provide color long into fall. (They love all colors in dahlias, except for red or yellow.)

It's easy to see how the garden, which wraps around the house and barn in a wonderful fashion, has influenced these two in their interior design. It's also easy to see how it has inspired them in their business. Many of the products that the duo has designed have their roots in the West Sussex countryside, such as the bamboo planter, the cushions featuring images of foliage, leaves, and twigs, and the urns that are perfect for the current style of Dutch Old Master floral bouquets. "Our garden constantly inspires and influences our designs, from our furniture collections to our homewares."

Above and following spread: Moschino and Vergeylen took great joy in juxtaposing boxwood pruned to look like balls with the straight lines of the garden. The different shapes create a visual pattern of forms that bring to mind the designs in fabric.

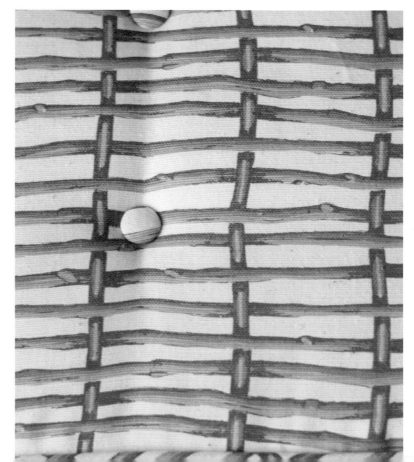

Opposite and this page: Known for their sophisticated interiors, Moschino and Vergeylen don't appear to be the dirt-on-hands gardening types, yet their elegant West Sussex house is a tribute to their horticultural talents. Clipped boxwood, antique statuary, and perfect parterres are testament to their gardening skills. They have also started designing and selling garden-inspired pieces, ranging from textiles and urns to furniture, in their store Nicholas Haslam in Pimlico, London.

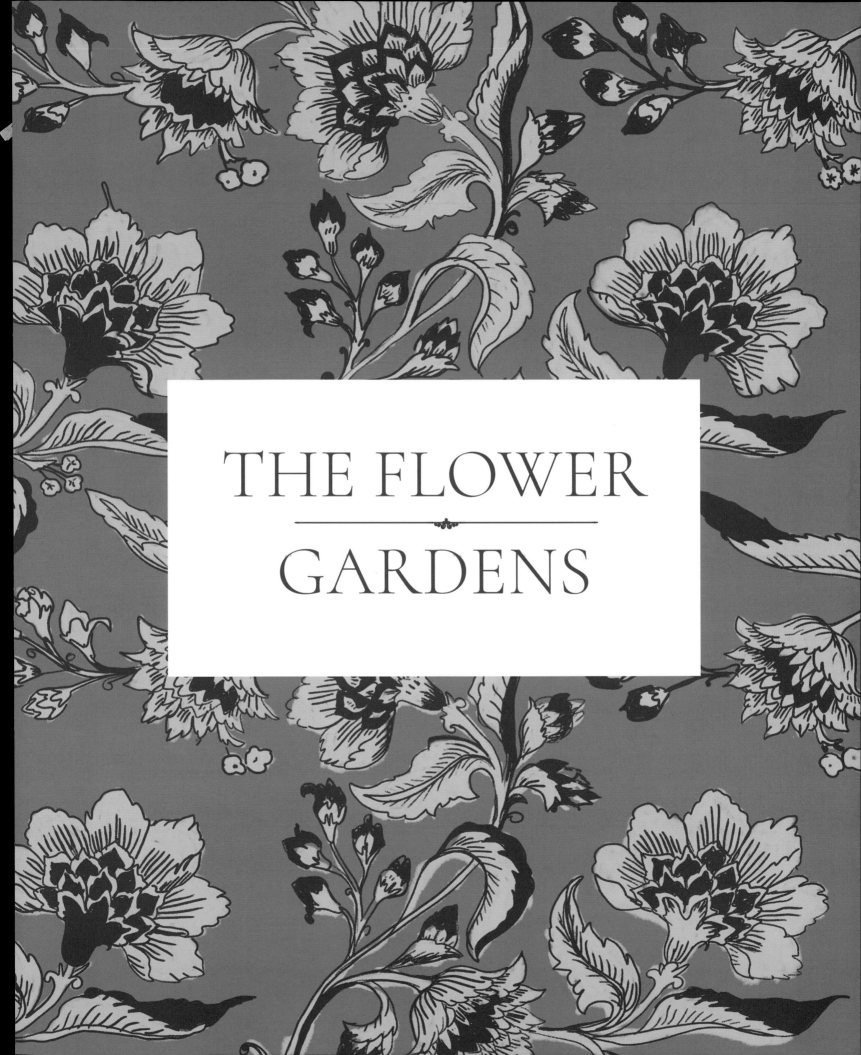

THE FLOWER
GARDENS

CHRISTIAN DIOR

Normandy

At the turn of the last century, a young Christian Dior wandered the garden paths of his family's villa, Les Rhumbs, on the coast of Normandy in France. It was his mother Madeleine's garden but he had helped create it, drawing on his emerging artistic talent expressed in his love of color, form, line, layers, scent, and texture, and the feelings they aroused in him. There, among the spring tulips and rose beds, the romantic pergola and the maritime pines, his lifelong passions for gardening and fashion design were formed.

If he had not become a couturier, Dior would have made a fine landscape designer. Dior showed interest in gardens from a young age. He knew the Latin names of many plants by the age of twelve, and spent much of his time engrossed in Vilmorin-Andrieux gardening catalogs. (Later, when he designed his spring/summer 1952 collection, he named a dress after the mail-order seed and plant company as a quiet acknowledgment of the childhood debt he owed to them.) "I was happiest in the company of plants and flower beds," he wrote in one of his memoirs.

Working alongside his mother when he could, usually between school lessons and on weekends, Dior took on increasing responsibility for the flower beds in Les Rhumbs's garden, and later supervised the construction of a pergola, a water garden with a reflecting pond, and a rose garden on the cliff. Inspired by British garden designer Gertrude Jekyll, he incorporated many of her ideas. For example, he instructed that the perennial beds be left an irregular shape—he felt the look beautifully captured the poetry of wildflowers growing along the nearby country lanes.

Above: Much of Christian Dior's iconography stems from his childhood garden in Normandy, and his abiding love for the flower beds there. Opposite: Dior cultivated this garden, alongside his mother, Madeleine, and then he transposed his love of flowers to his dresses when he became a couturier.

His mother had envisioned an English-style park to match the Anglo-Norman villa and its elegant facade. But Dior had a good eye for design, even then, and integrated more flowers, which pleased his mother. He was particularly fond of roses and lilies of the valley, which remained his favorites.

This early education in the garden, alongside his more formal academic one, soon began to shape Dior's senses and develop his aesthetics, especially his eye for color and silhouette. (He had clearly inherited excellent taste from his mother who believed that "life must be a work of art.") Young Dior even came to love the color of the family home—a pale pebble pink and gray, which became his preferred colors in his couture.

These years, surrounded by the beauty of flowers in the French countryside, helped to forge the future couturier's creativity. Everything in Dior's adult life dated back to this garden. He spent years trying to re-create its beauty, poetry, and magic and was sentimental about it until the day he died. For him, the garden represented his refuge, a temple of calm and contemplation. It was possibly also a link to his mother, who died of grief when Dior's brother was struck down by an incurable disease. (A year later, in 1931, the family's fortune was lost due to the financial crash of 1929.) Dior kept a photo album of his childhood garden in his bedroom for the rest of his life. The property was later sold. But in 1997, the House of Dior bought it back and transformed it into the Christian Dior Museum, dedicated to the couturier, his career, and his childhood years.

The flowers at Les Rhumbs became the inspiration when Dior, seeking to establish himself as a couturier, began to sketch a new silhouette for women's clothing in his Paris studio. In postwar France and beyond, women longed for something different to dress in, something that would transport them out of their trauma and into a new state of sartorial delight. Dior gave it to them, with gowns whose silhouettes came directly from his childhood garden. He hoped the poetry of petals would restore their spirits. And it did. When Dior asked Rébé, the esteemed embroidery house, to create simple, fresh embroideries for him to work with, the textiles they conceived and the creations Dior made with them were so ravishing, and so different from anything that had come before, that the previous demand for Oriental patterns went straight out the door. Women immediately began dressing in botanical-inspired designs instead.

Opposite: Many of Dior's outfits, such as this one, a gown called *May* from the spring/summer 1953 collection, were inspired by this garden, and even the descriptions of the dresses evoked a garden in summer. He once wrote: "Each new collection is like a new spring, with the pieces of fabric as new shoots." Above: Two spectacular parts of the garden, which was restored by Guillaume Pellerin in 2002.

Above left: The silk *Porcelaine* evening dress from the Haute Couture spring/ summer 1958 *Trapeze* line, designed by Yves Saint Laurent during his time at the House of Dior, reflects the pale peach-pink tone of Dior's childhood home, right, and its pink and peach roses. Above right: Dior's life became a pattern of flowers, in both work and life. He surrounded himself with blooms. They awakened his creative senses and gave him ideas for fashion collections, year after year. Opposite: The process of restoring Dior's childhood home on the coast of Normandy took several years. Once it was done, work began on the garden's flower and rose beds, which he and his mother had loved so much.

In the years to come, Dior designed collections that looked as if they'd sprung from his garden beds. Indeed, the decade between 1947 and 1957 was dominated by floral motifs. He named more than fifty gowns after roses. His collections and catwalk shows looked like moving bouquets of beauty. These garments were more akin to a garden of flora than elegant folds of fabric. As fashion historian Farid Chenoune wrote in the book *Dior Impressions*, "It could be said that [Dior] was the head gardener of this revival; its inspired horticulturalist."

Among the many feminine, voluminous, floral-decorative dresses that Dior designed, his favorites included *Corolle* (spring/summer 1947 and autumn/fall 1947), *Tulipe* (spring/summer 1953), and *Muguet* (spring/summer 1954)—the last being French for "lily of the valley." Many of these pieces featured enormous spreading skirts, with the fullness of a just-opened rose; or intricate, elongated layers like graceful leaves; or delicate embroidery reminiscent of vines, sprigs, branches, and garlands, cascading around the waist and up over the bustier. Sometimes tiny meadow flowers or lily of the valley were stitched inside hem linings, or petals and stamens were rendered in minute detail in discreet corners of dresses. Even Dior's colors had botanical references: pink was begonia, mauve

was azalea, blue was hydrangea, and yellow was daffodil. Dior wanted to make women feel as though they were "blooming" with joy. He wanted them to feel as if they were in the paradise of their own secret gardens.

In 1949, using money raised from his successful collections, Dior bought his first home, a mill called Le Moulin du Coudret, in Milly-la-Forêt, south of Paris, where he quietly traded his gray striped suits for a simple gardener's outfit of rubber boots and a Russian peasant's hat. The house was in a ruined state, set in a swamp, but Dior set about transforming it. He worked on weekends to drain the swamp and clear the undergrowth. Once he had done that, he began creating the garden, although he was always conscious that the property should retain its simple charm. He wanted it to look like a peasant's garden.

Slowly, this country refuge became Dior's second studio, a creative workshop where he plundered the garden for ideas. Nature was again his muse. He looked to it for inspiration, especially for forms, fragrances, color palettes, and unexpected relationships, which he felt Mother Nature did better than any designer. "After women, flowers are the most lovely thing [*sic*] God has given the world," he once wrote.

Opposite: The restored garden beds at the Christian Dior Museum feature pinky-purple tulips in spring. Above: A rhododendron bush in a blush shade and a row of standard roses reflect Dior's love of both roses and the color pink.

A few years later, in 1951, he purchased another villa in the South of France, called La Colle Noire, where he again tried to re-create the beauty of his childhood garden, albeit in a much different setting. "I could go right back to my roots and discover, in another climate, the closed garden that protected my childhood," he later recalled. One of the first things he did was to ask his gardeners to plant jasmine as far as the eye could see.

Before Christian Dior died in October 1957, he asked that his coffin be covered in flowers. Beneath a profusion of camellias, tuberoses, hawthorn blossoms, and lilies of the valley, whose white spring bells appeared droopier than usual, as if in deep mourning, Dior took his final bow.

When responsibility for the House of Dior passed on to subsequent creative directors and designers, most of them were,

interestingly, gardeners themselves. Marc Bohan, Gianfranco Ferré, and John Galliano were all keen green thumbs who—like Dior—often designed their Dior collections and catwalk shows with floral motifs. Raf Simons proved to be equally talented at dressing women in pretty petals: his first Dior collection included double-faced dresses, one side strewn with traditionally embroidered flowers and the other with contemporary floral ornaments. Current designer Maria Grazia Chiuri continues this tradition, creating dresses with discreet bouquets of hand-dyed silk petals and orchestrating shows that feel like secret gardens.

If there is a Heaven and Dior has gone to it, which seems likely given how much pleasure he brought to people and cared about the earth, then it's also likely that Heaven is a garden, and if it is, Dior is in the right place. What's more, he's probably out, pruning the roses and tending to the perennials.

Opposite: The view of the sea from the garden—and the hues of the landscape—influenced the palette of many of Dior's dresses and collections. Many of the elements that he designed are still in the garden at the family villa (now the Christian Dior Museum). The garden has been restored in recent years, along with the rest of the property. Above: A Dior dress from the Haute Couture spring/summer 1953 *Tulipe* line.

Opposite: Dior's *Muguet* dress, inspired by the flower lily of the valley, from the Haute Couture spring/summer 1957 *Libre* line. Above, left: One of Dior's favorite blooms was lily of the valley. Above, right: The entrance to his garden on the coast of Normandy.

CAROLYNE ROEHM

Connecticut

In the northwest corner of Connecticut, there is a diminutive village called Sharon. Sharon is so understated and beautifully muted in its landscape that you could easily drive through without noticing its true beauty. One of the few indications that it's a place of horticultural significance is a series of small signs that pop up in spring, stating, rather enticingly: "GARDENS THIS WAY." If you follow these signs to the estates beyond, you'll soon discover that this area is an Arcadia where gardens have been elevated to an art form. Flowers are not just revered here; they are celebrated—at fairs and garden festivals, in photogenic nurseries and bucolic farm stalls, and even in books, of which there are a surprising number that feature local people and places. "Gardening is our sport," a local once quipped. "People garden here like other people play tennis."

One of these flower lovers is Carolyne Roehm. Formerly a fashion designer and now textile designer, artist, and author of more than twelve best-selling books, Roehm resides in a beguiling idyll called Weatherstone, a gracious, 1765 Georgian manor purchased with her former husband more than thirty years ago, before the area had reached the radar of Manhattan.

The interiors of Weatherstone are impressive, especially since Roehm restored them following a devastating fire in 1999. Roehm refined the rooms to emphasize their elegant Georgian forms. She also opened up the drawing room to make a two-story great room with a magnificent wrap-around mezzanine, now filled with blue-and-white china, gilded antique furniture, and unusual wooden chandeliers created by artisans.

Above: The formal rose garden in front of Weatherstone's gracious facade. Opposite: Peonies, one of Carolyne Roehm's favorite flowers, growing in the perennial garden.

However, it is in the garden where Roehm's talents truly come to the fore. Like the house, Weatherstone's garden is a place of quiet grace. It resembles a living painting of flower beds and neatly symmetrical hedges. There is a clear sense of architectural dignity here, in the buildings as well as in the structured garden borders. But there is also a swaying sensuality to the planting scheme, which incorporates swaths of scented hyacinths and long-legged tulips in spring, lush roses in summer, and all kinds of herbaceous borders that bloom in high spirits until the end of September.

All good gardens need to have an underlying order, and Weatherstone's green rooms sit neatly in a plan that begins with a parterre and ends with a walled garden and Victorian greenhouse. The parterre, says Roehm, forms the structured part of the garden, with its stern lines and strict axes. It was designed to reflect the elegant grandeur of the historic residence beyond, particularly the great room with its soaring ceiling and handsome proportions. But the geometric lines of the parterre also create a clearly defined relationship between house and garden. Anchored by Sargent crabapples, the parterre fills with hundreds of tulips in the spring. While these tulips soften this part of the garden, there is still a sense of order and grace here. Even the beds seem innately well mannered.

There is also an allée flanked by rows of trees in this part of the garden, which leads the eye out into the landscape. And there is an abundant rose garden, too, which is festooned with blooms in summer and offers unlimited picking opportunities—and the raw material for Roehm's beloved photo shoots and books.

Opposite and above: The rose garden was Roehm's first formal garden at Weatherstone, and erupts into bloom in June. It has been the setting for many summer dinners. Favorite roses include Constance Spry, Peace, and Lady of Megginch. "I love so many many flowers," she says. "But if I could only have a few flowers, I simply could never choose between scented garden roses and my beloved peonies."

Roehm's favorite color palette for the garden is the feminine, romantic shades of purples and delicate pinks, but she also adores bolder colors, such as oranges, and the almost black of some tulips. Her choice varieties include the beautiful Green Wave, Foxtrot, Flair, and the patterned Estella Rinjnveld.

Above top: The perennial garden in full floraison. Left: Hyacinths in the cutting garden. Above: Plans for the tulip and allium beds. Opposite: The tulip garden in full spring bloom.

More informal gardens are on the opposite side of the house. This is perhaps where the garden's real delights are found—certainly its biggest surprises. Venture through the restored Victorian greenhouse, which Roehm worked on a great deal herself, and you come to the white trellis-fence that invites a view of the enormous profusion of what's inside. Filled with endless rows of flower beds, which include sweet hyacinths that scent the air for weeks in early spring, it's a pragmatic harvest garden made for flowers that are meant to be cut (tulips and alliums follow the hyacinths). It's also a spectacular space that has a dreamy quality, as if disconnected from the real world.

The cutting garden flows into a second one created for perennials, which accommodates even more of Roehm's beloved blooms in big, overflowing herbaceous borders. Here, Roehm grows irises, salvia, alliums, lupine, and nepeta in soft palettes of mauve, pink, purple, and white. Elsewhere on the fifty-nine-acre estate, there is a walled garden, a pool garden, more rose beds, a grand potager, and a lake. Together it seems like a lot to manage, and Roehm admits it is a handful. But the sum of these parts creates a magnificent tableau. Despite the impressive size, it is a garden on a human scale, designed to be lived in and loved, where one can drift between borders to pick, plant, plan, or simply revel in the scents of spring and summer.

Roehm admits that when she first arrived at Weatherstone, she wanted to emulate the great French and Italian gardens, with their manicured sophistication. But over the years, as both she and the garden have matured, she has drifted to the more romantic and looser-planted style of English flower gardens. Even the potager, once modeled on the great kitchen gardens of Villandry and Versailles, has become a place for pulling out the pumpkins and planting tulips en masse, including Queen of the Night and the dramatic Rembrandt.

The perennial garden adjoins the cutting garden, and is more free-flowing in design, with mixed beds of bearded irises, peonies, salvia, nepeta, and roses planted in dedicated rows. The iris varieties include Victoria Falls, Cantina, and Rosalie Figg.

As much as it all looks effortless and easy, Roehm concedes that some things have not succeeded—delphiniums, for example, have not done well. And that sometimes she buys more plants at nurseries than she has space for. But these are minor things and all gardeners have experienced them. Looking at Weatherstone's beds, it's difficult to believe Roehm didn't study horticulture at an advanced level. But Roehm has always had an eye for design, so it's only natural that she feels at home within the fine lines and forms of a garden. She began her career as a fashion designer, first under the tutelage of Oscar de la Renta. Later she started her own label. Her greatest love, next to gardening and architecture, has always been textiles. Weatherstone is filled with exquisite woven silks and velvets, which sit easily alongside all the more rustic gardenalia. One of Roehm's current projects involves designing finely embroidered linen with the highly regarded Charmajesty brand.

Another current collaboration involves botanical dinnerware. But in recent years, she has also been doing her own artwork; her latest book features some of her beautiful watercolors.

Weatherstone has been good to Roehm. She restored it following the fire and it has sheltered and inspired her in turn. In her most recent book *At Home in the Garden*, she quoted Frank Lloyd Wright, who said, "Study nature, love nature, stay close to nature. It will never fail you." Weatherstone is a perfect example of the harmony that results when there is a good relationship between nature and man. Or in this case, woman, as this is very much a feminine garden. It is a superlative account of Roehm's love affair with flowers, chronicled in an ever-changing narrative of blossoms, blooms, and beauty.

Opposite: Roehm draws on her garden and home for inspiration in her various collections and collaborations. Above: Roehm's great love for blue and white in her home and garden has been the impetus for a new line of blue notecards and prints (available through carolyneroehm.com), as well as embroidered blue-and-white linen for Charmajesty Linens.

Opposite, above, and following spread: Roehm restored the Victorian
greenhouse herself, with the help of a small team. It is now used for growing
beautiful geraniums, violas, and pansies, which thrive in the warmth and shelter.
The potting shed adjoining the greenhouse is a mini gallery devoted to botanical
prints that Roehm has collected over the years, as well as garden antiques.

This page: Amid the vibrant pinks, mauves, and plums of the flower gardens, there is room at Weatherstone for quiet green and white. This is most apparent in the Victorian greenhouse but Roehm also likes the elegance of white tulips, geraniums, and the sophisticated structure of white obelisks in the potager. Opposite: Topiaries and boxwood are overwintered in the colder months.

BUNNY WILLIAMS & JOHN ROSSELLI

Connecticut

Each May a glamorous gathering of gardeners descends on the small village of Sharon, Connecticut. They form a society that's usually only seen at places like the Chelsea Flower Show. You can find this group by following the Hunter Wellingtons, natty hats, and perfectly pressed linen shirts along Hosier Road. Or you can look for their white marquees, chic wicker baskets and straw bags, and stalls piled so high with pretty vintage linen you'd think you were in Provence. This, for those not familiar with the gardening calendar, is the annual two-day Trade Secrets garden fair, one of the most stylish social outings in the gardening set's schedule. It's where they get to "talk dirty" for a day or two—a botany boot camp for the well-heeled or "well-Wellingtoned."

Most come for the conversation as much as for the rare plants and rustic garden tools on display. If Ralph Lauren were to do a collection called A Connecticut Garden, this could well be the photo shoot. With the sun dancing upon the artfully clipped bay trees and the smell of new spring bulbs in the air, it's an intoxicating scene.

The fair was founded by the renowned New York interior designer and textile designer Bunny Williams to raise money for Women's Support Services, a local charity, while promoting her favorite pastime—and that, it seems, of most of the locals. A decade after it began, Trade Secrets has become so successful that tickets for the 8:00 a.m. entry are snapped up immediately. Regulars include Martha Stewart and Carolyne Roehm. During his life, Oscar de la Renta was also a fan.

The fair is only part of the annual weekend's festivities. In addition, five local gardeners open their gates to visitors. These gardens change every year with the exception of one, which is always included: the garden of Manor House, the weekend

Above: The front facade of Manor House. Opposite: The house's flagstone sun porch offers comfortable seating surrounded by topiaries, clipped boxwood, and other plants.

retreat of Williams and her husband, antiques dealer, John Rosselli. This is because it's arguably one of the most beautiful private gardens in the state, if not New England. People trek to Connecticut to see Manor House as much as they do to shop for antique daisy grubbers and linen pinafores.

Manor House is located in Falls Village, a quiet hamlet of a few dignified streets and historical buildings painted every shade of New England white. Built in 1840, the gracious residence is reached via an enchanting tree-lined driveway and surrounded by a tapestry of intertwined gardens so delightful that you itch to Instagram them. It's a place with so much personality that when Williams wrote a book about it, *An Affair with a House*, it immediately became an international best seller.

The home didn't always look like this. When Williams first saw the grand but neglected house, more than thirty years ago, it appeared more like the world's end than *Howard's End*. But she saw the potential and set about transforming it. When she met Rosselli, he became equally enamored with it. Now the couple spends most weekends there. Williams says it is her "refuge." (The couple also owns residences in Manhattan and the Dominican Republic.)

Embellished with a Southern-style, double-lattice porch (which originally wrapped three sides of the dwelling), the house is an anomaly in this area of primarily Greek Revival architecture. It looks as if it belongs in the South (the original owner built it for his wife, who came from there). When Williams first saw it, she recognized its fine "bones" and knew immediately that, despite the drab and slightly dilapidated interior and unkempt grounds, she could create a comfortable but sophisticated country retreat there. But then, design comes naturally to this energetic decorator. Over the decades, she has taken her hand to everything from fabric to

furniture design either in collaboration with others or through the collections produced under her eponymous brand, Bunny Williams Home. Indeed, one only needs to wander outside, into the garden, to see Williams's talent.

Manor House has many gardens, even for a substantial country residence. Williams's first garden here was located on the south side of the house, where she replaced an old tennis court with a sunken garden. This was eventually enclosed by boxwood terraces on the inside and towering hedges on the outside, and anchored by pairs of ornamental sculptures, with a koi pond in the center. The flagstaff terrace and the wide steps leading down to it, edged in mauve hydrangeas in summer, made this area feel like an outdoor "room." Now further enhanced by scented lilac hedges and swaying alliums during the summer months, it offers a delightful view from the house's enclosed porch and is a wonderful place to escape to.

On the other side of the barn is a different garden altogether—an enormous kitchen garden, inspired by the potager at Villandry. Williams returned from a trip to France enthused by the idea of creating a similar vegetable garden; it is now her husband who tends it, growing herbs and produce for his culinary creations. He and Williams have good-natured debates about what to plant, but Williams always manages to slip a few flowers in among the vegetable beds.

In 2015, she had success with the tulip Sensual Touch, a pretty apricot-colored tulip variety that resembles roses. Most summers there are snapdragons and zinnias, rosemary and thyme, and of course dahlias. There is a greenhouse here, too, which is perhaps the busiest building on the property. ("I can always tell who the real gardeners are because they want to see my greenhouse," she once told me.)

The first garden that Williams created at Manor House was the formal sunken garden, which was carved out of an old tennis court. While this garden offers a beautiful vista from the sun porch, it is equally lovely standing on the terrace looking up at the grand old home. The stone steps create a dramatic focal point, like a stage set. The enormous pitted blue hydrangeas on both sides of the steps reflect the tones of the garden's color palette. Following spread: Alliums and salvias punctuate the formal sunken garden with purple exclamation marks in the summer months.

And there is the parterre garden, which has become renowned in gardening circles for its elegant beauty and charming conservatory. Lined by twelve-foot-high hornbeam hedges on one side and an endearing post-and-rail timber fence on the other, it is divided into a geometric grid of clipped boxwood and planted in a different color palette each year. In the spring, when tulips fill the space, it is a sublime sight of swaying petals.

The garden at Manor House has influenced the couple's lives in more ways than one. Their previous shop, the Manhattan store Treillage, was a paean to garden-inspired pieces, from ceramics to furniture. (Williams's new store, Bunny Williams Home, on East 59th Street, is proving just as popular with the design set.) And inside Manor House, there is also evidence of its gentle impact on the couple's lives and living spaces. Potted topiary trees punctuate the living room, lettuceware rests on the tabletops, and the dining room is papered in a historic green-and-white stripe the exact shade of the Connecticut woods in late summer.

To bring the outside in, the kitchen was expanded to allow for a bank of large windows overlooking the garden. Elsewhere inside the house, the hall's Irish console table is always filled with huge floral arrangements, while botanical textiles or painted flowers decorate curtains, cushions, pillows, and furniture, such as a pretty eighteenth-century chest of drawers painted with delicate blooms in the style of decorative artist Angelica Kauffmann.

Perhaps the most obvious sign of the influence of the garden on the interiors is in the former barn, now a superb entertaining space and guest quarters. Also built in 1840, this barn was used for storage before Rosselli decided it would make a wonderful place to house guests, and set about redesigning it to accommodate them—and himself, with an office in the corner.

The wooden gate entrance to the parterre garden features geometric beds of boxwood that fill with tulips in spring. Beyond is the conservatory, which forms part of the converted barn, now grand guest quarters and a garden library.

Now there is a handsome bedroom encased in the former hayloft, a delightful bathroom with botanical prints, and a spectacular great room with soaring, twenty-two-foot-high ceilings that features an extensive library of new and vintage gardening titles. There is a flower room in the corner, with an old copper butler's sink and open shelving containing vases, vessels, and zinc watering cans. Potted plants dot the benchtop, creating a scene that makes visitors on Open Days exclaim with envy.

It seems entirely natural that a flower room has been placed next to this great room, given that both lead out to the conservatory. This indoor-outdoor space, a stunning annex to the barn,

developed when Williams found three arched windows in an antiques shop on Route 7, which had come from another house, built circa 1840, located along the Hudson River. With the addition of skylights, antique French terra-cotta tiles on the floor, a huge stone table, and a long stone side table for plants, the building blossomed into a beautiful conservatory, and then into an atmospheric entertaining space. Here guests dine surrounded by lush ferns and foliage while looking out to the formal parterre and its beds of tulips and flowers. In this room the garden truly merges with the interior in a seamless, easy pairing of plants and people. It is no wonder that guests find it difficult to leave after a dinner party has drawn to a close.

Above: The conservatory's dining area surrounded by potted ferns.
Opposite: The parterre garden view from inside.

Many similarities exist between gardens and design. Both are about scale and structure, colors and layers, and textures. Interior designers and architects seem to have a natural talent for creating outdoor spaces. Manor House is a wonderful example. It is a home where the interiors and the garden have not only influenced one another but have become almost indistinguishable. Boundaries between the two are so seamless in certain areas—particularly in rooms such as the porch, terrace, conservatory, and barn—that you can drift between them without noticing whether you are inside, or out.

At Manor House, Williams and Rosselli have created the seemingly impossible: a home and a garden that mix formality with easy living, and whimsicality with classical elements. It's also a place that provides them with endless inspiration for their designs and creations. This country garden is a magnificent muse for their life, art, style, and design.

Opposite: A bouquet of fresh flowers from the garden. During the garden's flowering months, Williams and her gardeners take delight in filling her many vases with magnificent blooms. Above, left: A comfortable sofa offers guests a place to sit in the converted barn turned guest quarters. Above, right: Detail of a guest bedroom. Following spread: The parterre garden.

Opposite: An oversized urn anchors one of the geometric beds in the formal parterre garden. This page: The garden at Manor House has influenced Williams in more ways than one. She and John Rosselli owned the renowned Manhattan store Treillage Ltd. for twenty-five years, which was a paean to garden-inspired pieces, from ceramics to furniture. Williams's new store and showroom, Bunny Williams Home, on East Fifty-ninth Street in New York City, has equally beautiful products inspired by flora and foliage, from textiles to lamps, cushions, and pillows. As well, her collaborations with other brands and companies, such as Lee Jofa, often result in products in which the patterns, textures, colors, lines, or layers are inspired by the verdant corners of this country garden.

Opposite: Many of Williams and Rosselli's objets d'art are inspired by the garden, including hurricane lamps with leafy hems, metal ivy entwined around the potting shed taps in the antique copper sink, and gourd-shaped ceramics. Above: Williams's new design studio is an airy, light-filled space with picture windows framing the view of the Connecticut landscape at one end, and a huge fireplace at the other end. Along one wall are bookshelves to hold the designer's enormous collection of design, architecture, and garden books.

Opposite and above: Williams's potager was inspired by the grand potagers in France. It is used for growing both vegetables and flowers, and provides the couple with abundant produce.

AERIN LAUDER

Hamptons

Hamptons residents are serious about their hedges and their garden beds. They tend to be house proud (or should that be horticulturally proud?) about what lies beyond their privet hedges and picket fences. They also tend to spend a lot of time in their gardens, particularly during the summer months. Some will even happily get their hands dirty, toiling away in their flower beds. To relax, return to nature, pour a drink, look over the glorious landscapes, and remember what leisure and fresh air feel like.

Aerin Lauder is a perfect example of this lifestyle. The designer, global creative director of the Estée Lauder Companies and head of AERIN, her own fast-growing empire, spends most weekends at her home in the Hamptons and admits that it's her sanctuary. She finds a welcome stillness here, between the ocean and the vineyards; a quietude that comes from being out in the country, with that fine Hamptons light and fresh air. One of the ways she achieves tranquility is by going out into the garden first thing each morning to "gather flowers for the house."

The late fashion designer Oscar de la Renta once wrote that "a garden is probably the most spiritual and pure of joys that one is ever likely to encounter." Lauder seems to have discovered this, too. It feels instantly calming to be around her here, on this serene, green estate on the South Fork of Long Island. Even after driving for three hours in Friday traffic.

Above: The rooms of Aerin Lauder's Hamptons home are always filled with fresh flowers. Opposite: The garden is a mix of mature trees, lawn, flower beds, and quiet corners. There is also a small picking garden.

One of the reasons for this bucolic bliss could be the abundance of blue hues. There is every kind of blue here, among the gentle greenery, from iris blue to delphinium blue to the pale shade of the sea after a storm has passed. The blues tend to be on the soft side—there is no intense Yves Klein blue. Colette once said, "There are connoisseurs of blue, just as there are connoisseurs of white," and Lauder seems to have inherited her famous grandmother Estée's love of the color. And why not, when it is one of the few shades that never dates? (Blue lovers don't need to argue this point. But if there is any question about it, one just needs to see Estée's old bedroom, which is still wallpapered in the same blue Pierre Frey print, Toile de Nantes, and looks just as fresh as it did decades ago.)

Blue is also the theme of the dining room, where antique Delft vases are displayed on wall brackets. And Estée's famous blue-and-white living room shimmers with walls painted in a pale Lutyens lilac (a custom mix by Donald Kaufman), which offers an unexpected but surprisingly beautiful backdrop for the Chinese and Japanese porcelain. Estée's favorite navy sofa, which rests in front of the delicately colored wall, creates a scene that brings to mind the multi-blue-hued interiors by celebrated British designer David Collins, who loved the combination of periwinkle and navy. (Collins used a similar lilac blue for his Blue Bar in London. Exacting in his practice, he once employed seventeen different shades of blue to achieve the desired effect.)

Blue reigns out in the garden, too, where the huge banks of mauve hydrangeas create impressionistic splashes of color in the lush green garden. It's easy to see how Lauder could be so influenced by the moods and hues of this gentle seaside hideaway, which includes collections of hats and wicker chaise lounges and piles of enticing books. The house and garden serve as an ever-changing moodboard. "I do find a lot of inspiration here for my designs," she concedes. "The palettes of my garden and house are dominant in my collections. There are always pieces each year that have an emphasis on blue, white, and purple."

Summer hydrangeas in the side garden inspire many of the hues in Aerin Lauder's AERIN designs and collections.

Above and opposite, top: Estée Lauder's famous blue-and-white room has changed little since she lived here, but her granddaughter Aerin Lauder has introduced new versions of her grandmother's beloved Chinese ginger jars on the fireplace mantel. Right: Estée and Aerin Lauder's love of flowers is reflected in many of the botanical motifs that Aerin Lauder uses in her products, including this textile for Lee Jofa. "I use a lot of floral prints in my fabric collections," she says. Indeed, many of the elements of the interior and garden, from the color palette to the floral motifs, show up in the AERIN collections. Blue is a dominant color, in both the house and garden. Following spread: A large bouquet of white hydrangeas brightens the library, with its striking chocolate walls and leopard-print sofa.

Other elements of this place that she takes design cues from are the flora and foliage that grow profusely in the garden. "Flowers have always been a great source of inspiration for me, and a big part of the AERIN brand," she says. "I use a lot of floral prints in my fabric collections, and also my candles." (The AERIN store in Southampton is a veritable bouquet of printed products, from pretty sundresses to hostess gifts.)

Flowers certainly take center stage at this estate, both outside and inside the residence. Rooms are filled with fresh blooms, and floral motifs can be seen throughout the house on wallpaper, textiles, cushions, china, and in paintings and prints. Follow the

petals—and the fragrances—and you can find yourself drifting from the grand hall to the library to the sunroom, and then out to the lawn and the interconnecting garden rooms until you end up at a spectacular all-white pool house inspired by one photographed by Slim Aarons, where even the white chandelier is shaped like ethereal branches and the white cushions feature tiny white flowers. This is a property where flowers are a priority. You can clearly see that a garden lover lives here.

Estée Lauder was also a fan of flowers and gardens, and her love for this place was such that when Aerin Lauder inherited the property, she left it "exactly as it was" for several years, reluctant

Opposite: The rooms of Aerin Lauder's Hamptons home are always filled with fresh flowers, some picked from her cutting garden and some sourced at nearby farm stands and florists. Favorites include roses, dahlias, peonies, morning glories, and of course hydrangeas. Above: The sunroom features wicker furniture in a natural palette. The fabric reflects the flowers grown in the cutting garden beyond.

to change her grandmother's taste and decorations. But then, slowly, Aerin Lauder began to make her own mark, and one of the major changes was commissioning well-known garden designer Perry Guillot to update the landscaping.

Transformed with a design that was part formal and part romantic ramble, the garden now winds around the house and the great old trees in an effortless, easygoing, welcoming fashion, beckoning visitors to explore.

Guillot also planted a cutting garden filled with hydrangeas, roses, dahlias, and peonies, which Lauder uses daily. (She also loves to visit the local farmers' markets for different kinds of blooms.)

Lauder's love for her garden also shows up in her collaborations with other brands and companies such as Lee Jofa (fabrics and rugs) and Lenox (china). Lauder admits that her earliest memories involve flowers—even when the house was owned by her grandmother, it was filled with vases of roses and tuberoses—and she continues to decorate it that way. Indeed, she seems to live her life surrounded by flowers, and treats them with the same care as she does her dogs, her children, and her business. (Lauder is hands-on. She brought out the vases for the book's photo shoot and made the arrangements herself.)

This house may be a weekend retreat, but Lauder always makes sure that it is filled with flowers, people and laughter, and food and conversation. All of it combines to create a beautiful tapestry of the memories of life.

Now, as she moves forward with her empire AERIN, building on her successful Southampton shop, Lauder will lean on the peace this enchanting hideaway provides more than ever before. And it, in turn, will no doubt continue to be a captivating muse.

The formal garden features a fountain surrounded by white roses and clipped boxwood. Following spread: The pool and pool house are the family's favorite places to relax and entertain in the summer months. A table set under the shade of an enormous tree for a summer luncheon features wicker tableware from Aerin Lauder's own collection, as well as a few pieces from other designers.

The pool house was inspired by Slim Aarons's famous photograph of Babe Paley in Jamaica, leaning on a pillar in her pool house. It opens on both sides to become a generous indoor-outdoor space. The garden's influence sneaks in via floral motifs on the cushions and pillows—a vintage fabric that Lauder re-created for Lee Jofa. The light fitting is a grand white chandelier shaped like branches.

BEN PENTREATH & CHARLIE McCORMICK

Dorset

The 1980s were famous for "It" girls, socialites and actresses who achieved fame by donning safety-pin frocks or filling magazine pages with their glamour and antics. In the Instagram age, there are "Insta" stars, and today they are business savvy. They own architecture firms. Or fashion labels. Or they write lifestyle blogs or cookbooks, and then launch their own magazine or TV show.

One of these modern Instagram identities is the engaging, energetic, and extraordinarily talented British architectural and interior designer Ben Pentreath. Pentreath has been in the design business for decades and found international fame via his blog and its witty depictions of his idyllic Dorset property, The Parsonage, which he shares with his husband, floral designer Charlie McCormick.

The Parsonage is an 1820s Regency house set in a cinematic green valley in West Dorset, two miles from the coast. Pentreath had long known of the house before he took on a lease in 2008; it had belonged to the family of his childhood friend, and some of his fondest memories were sown here, during summer visits.

Pentreath lived at The Parsonage for several years before meeting McCormick. (They also have a place in London—a flat in an old Georgian house in Bloomsbury, with a view out over the leafy square.) Bit by bit, the old parsonage received the Pentreath touch: the entrance was wallpapered in a striking Gothic print supplied by David Skinner of Dublin; antiques were bought, arranged, then rearranged; and rooms were decorated. Pentreath also painted the dining room Farrow & Ball's St. Giles Blue and lined it with Piranesi prints to create an eye-catching space.

Opposite: The spectacular dahlia hedge has become famous on Instagram. Above: The front facade of Ben Pentreath and Charlie McCormick's house looks over a tranquil wooded valley.

Filled with irresistible images of bucolic country life, Pentreath's blog posts about The Parsonage and other equally enviable homes led to two best-selling books, *English Decoration: Timeless Inspiration for the Contemporary Home* and *English Houses: Inspirational Interiors from City Apartments to Country Manor Houses*. In addition to all these projects he somehow also found time to write columns for the *Financial Review* and *House & Garden*. There is an interiors store, too, on Rugby Street, in London, called Pentreath & Hall. ("Hall" is retail partner Bridie Hall.)

Pentreath's artful depiction of this abundant lifestyle was so joyful, and filled with such humor and good taste, that it was no wonder people began to long for his Sunday evening blog posts. As Pentreath's readership grew, so too did his client list. Pentreath had already designed projects for H.R.H. The Prince of Wales, Liv Tyler, and Sarah Jessica Parker, among others, but the blog—and the books—attracted fans as far away as Australia.

Pentreath still regularly posts irresistible missives on social media about his friends' country residences, neoclassical architecture (one of his passions), family, travels with his partner, friends, and family, and London. But when he does a post about his Dorset garden, statistics skyrocket. The Parsonage is one of the most beloved gardens on Instagram. (Even Jasper Conran posts images including the giant dahlias he receives from Pentreath and McCormick.) One blog reader noted that the garden "needs its own Netflix series."

Pentreath is an accomplished gardener, but it is McCormick who has continued to enlarge and enrich the garden, gradually digging up more and more lawn for flower beds. Currently it includes three herbaceous borders and an enormous thirty-three yard-long dahlia and tulip bed.

The planting scheme is a blowsy, romantic, English style: sweet peas grow wildly over obelisks, huge rows of dahlias fall over their stakes, and glass cloches shelter new cucumbers. Everything is slightly overgrown and untamed in that appealing English-cottagey way. Along with spectacularly large dahlias and beautiful roses are alliums, foxgloves, poppies, bearded irises, snapdragons (McCormick's favorite is Appleblossom), sweet peas (Wiltshire Ripple and Almost Black), hollyhocks, Hidcote lavender, lilies (Tiger Babies), and dark, richly colored Raven penstemons.

Between all these blooms are billowy drifts of fennel, which fill out the wondrous floral arrangements McCormick makes (these often resemble bouquets painted by the Dutch Old Masters). In the potager, the flowers mix easily with the vegetables: there are runner beans and peas on hazel teepees and gorgeous, plump pumpkins that are so large they could be contenders for "Best Pumpkin" in the local village show. (McCormick is particularly talented at growing pumpkins.) In the spring, The Parsonage garden is at its most glorious, but it's also lovely in summer when Aphrodite and Pretty Jessica roses break into bloom.

The lovely entrance to the potager garden, a mix of flowers and vegetables. The thatched house on the neighbor's property, adds a charming backdrop.

While McCormick may be the gardener in the family, Pentreath looks to these colorful flower beds for design ideas and inspiration. The garden has become his go-to source and his interiors have become much more exuberant as a result. For example, the kitchen at The Parsonage went from having classic white walls to Farrow & Ball's Wet Sand (a saturated orange shade), then to a cheery, Colefax and Fowler–esque egg-yolk-yellow, which—either deliberately or coincidentally—matches the enormous dahlias growing outside the kitchen window. The pale pink sitting room—now the endearing, uplifting hue of a Dorset dawn—reflects the delicate pink flowers that unfurl in the herbaceous borders during the summer months,

as well as the climbing roses that twirl around the house's exterior. (The color, mixed by Papers and Paints in Chelsea, is now named Parsonage Pink.)

Pentreath's eye for nuances of color is so fine that when his paint colorist pops in with new samples of green for his boss to review, the interior designer grumbles good-naturedly about the challenges of finding "the exact shade." If Pentreath hadn't entered the world of architecture, he might have become a very fine artist. McCormick's sensitivity to color is also remarkable. He was the one who persuaded Pentreath to go bolder with his color choices. As a result, both The Parsonage and their London home are ongoing arias of color.

Above, left: Vintage garden books in The Parsonage's flower room. Above, right, and opposite: Pentreath is currently managing many projects for various clients, but it's his own Dorset home, The Parsonage, that has much of Instagram's design crowd talking, with its enormous beds of pink and yellow dahlias, planted and picked by Pentreath's husband, floral designer Charlie McCormick. The pink and yellow palette has inspired similar-hued rooms in both The Parsonage and other country cottages everywhere.

Left: The kitchen is painted egg-yolk yellow. Above, top and bottom:
Squash growing in the potager, and dahlias waiting in the flower room.

Above, top: The view out to the church, framed by geraniums. Above, left: A chair in one of the guest bedrooms. Above, right: Vintage books in the flower room. Opposite: The church glimpsed through the dahlia beds. Following spread: Dahlias as far as the eye can see in The Parsonage's dahlia hedge; a bouquet freshly picked on a September day; and Wellington boots by the door of the pink sitting room.

But horticulture offers these designers more than eye-catching hues. Flowers not only form the basis of their floral arrangements for home and business—botanicals also inform their fabric designs, prints, wrapping paper, and cards sold at the store.

The Parsonage has achieved global fame because it is a magical place; it is small enough to cultivate easily but large enough to

spread out with dahlia beds as far as the eye can see. With a delightful church and lake next door, plus its surrounding acres of green English hillsides, The Parsonage feels like a Merchant Ivory film brought to life. Blissful. Tranquil. And filled with beauty from one charming border to the other.

Above: Glass cloches lined up in the potager. Opposite: The potager at the end of summer, with its lush vegetable and flower beds.

GARY McBOURNIE & BILL RICHARDS

Nantucket

Nantucket is a theater set of remarkable architecture. The cobbled streets of town are dotted with Federalist and Greek Revival mansions, which sit neatly alongside beautifully preserved eighteenth- and nineteenth-century clapboard houses. Farther out of the town of Nantucket, the landscape is punctuated with beach houses ranging from notable architect-designed homes to quaint coastal cottages. One of these places, in a quiet area of the island known for its sandy roads and beach within reach, is the weekend home of interior designer Gary McBournie and his husband Bill Richards.

This is the fifth house that McBournie and Richards have owned on Nantucket. The interior designer has had great success restoring residences, as well as commercial projects on the island. Nantucket has been kind to him, career-wise. But it's this bold beach house that he and Richards feel most sentimental about. They plan to stay here. And that decision may have something to do with the enchanting garden.

McBournie is as passionate about gardens as he is about good design, and when he and Richards bought this formerly run-down house the first thing they did was to plant out the garden. "I believe in the French way: plan the landscaping first, then design the house. Our builders weren't happy, because they had to walk around it whenever they came in," he laughs. However, it was a prudent move, because it is now mature, and the privet hedges enclose the property to create the feeling of a secret sanctuary.

Above: The formal flower beds in front of Gary McBournie and Bill Richards's home. Opposite: The herringbone-patterned brickwork provides elegant paths, while also subtly referencing the bold orange palette in the house's interiors.

The effect of a *hortus conclusus* is further emphasized by the garden's location, which is set right behind the charming blue front gate, and the high hedges on either side of it. Visitors must walk through the boxwood-edged beds of Hidcote lavender, alliums, irises, and hydrangeas to enter the house—a clever strategy that slows people down, as they stop to smell the irises or exclaim at the hydrangeas. The four formal flower beds are centered around a circa-1890 sphere, a sculpture that immediately anchors the space. The elegant herringbone-patterned brickwork provides paths, and also references the bold orange palette of the home's interiors.

The garden has been planted with blue hydrangeas, sculptural irises, white alliums, alchemilla (lady's-mantle), and all manner of roses, peonies, and perennials in every shade of pink, mauve,

and orange. It looks like an Impressionist painting done with delicate brushstrokes and many daubs of Winsor & Newton paint. This is because McBournie and Richards and their gardener, Julie Wood, like to overplant, to create a painterly effect. It's a garden designed to be lived in and loved, and picked—a working garden as much as an elegantly designed one.

Indoors, the garden's influence is clearly seen. For example, the library's walls and door are upholstered in a soft, light green fabric echoing the color of new spring shoots. (The fabric is a custom green called Continents, by Bob Collins & Sons.) The dining room is also a serene paean to green, with chairs upholstered in Lee Jofa's Crosshatch in Apple Green, an unexpected but perfect companion for the room's gold walls (Champagne on Pewter Leaf, by Phillip Jeffries). Another

Opposite: McBournie and Richards chose this site because there is "great light" in this part of the island, which the house captures through every window. Above: A guest bedroom with floral wallpaper in a Bob Collins & Sons print.

Bob Collins fabric—floral this time, and in quieter shades of pale blue and tangerine—covers the walls of the guest bedroom, creating the effect of climbing roses and vines.

The main bedroom's colors are more intense but still clearly evoke the garden and the ocean. The saturated royal-blue hue matches the shade of the irises outside, while the addition of a dramatic Marimekko fabric called Räsymatto increases the space's glamour quotient. Part garden and part ocean, this unusual design scheme extends into the master bathroom, where brass Waterworks hardware has developed a lovely "shiplike" tarnish. The outdoor shower is enhanced with climbing vines and pots of flowers.

The kitchen also references the garden, with its cheerful painted checkerboard floors, done in Benjamin Moore's Racing Orange. (The tile pattern brings to mind the herringbone pattern of the orange bricks in the paths outside.)

Every room in this house has a vibrant personality. Even the enormous back porch is a cheerful, welcoming space, with old bamboo furniture from the 1940s and '50s that McBournie has had repainted in marine varnish.

This house is filled with the couple's humor and wit, but also shows a considered eye for connections between nature and design that marry indoor and outdoor spaces. It is a house that not only flows out to the garden but also brings it inside, through the use of eye-catching colors and textures and, of course, big bunches of fresh-picked flowers. Beach houses should encourage adventure and fun, both in design and in lifestyle. This spectacular retreat shows how wonderful boldness and creativity can be.

Above: The green library, with its upholstered walls, in a print by Bob Collins & Sons. Opposite: The guest cottage, which has a delightful look out over the garden.

Top, left: A bedroom reflects the hue of the hydrangeas in the garden. Top, right: One of McBournie's textile designs, produced with Antilles Design, a company in which he and Richards are partners. Left: A bouquet of summer roses. Above: The main living room features high ceilings and modern artwork, all in a palette of blue and tangerine. Opposite: The kitchen is a playful space that features an orange-checkered floor. Following spread: The glorious outdoor patio opens to the garden on all sides.

Top and right: The garden's planting scheme sees deep-purple spring irises
giving way to bright orange dahlias and serene blue hydrangeas in summer.
The color palette is not only the couple's favorite, it is so striking and delightful
that they have taken it inside, to create rooms and textiles of similar hues.
Above: One of McBournie's textile designs, produced with Antilles Design.

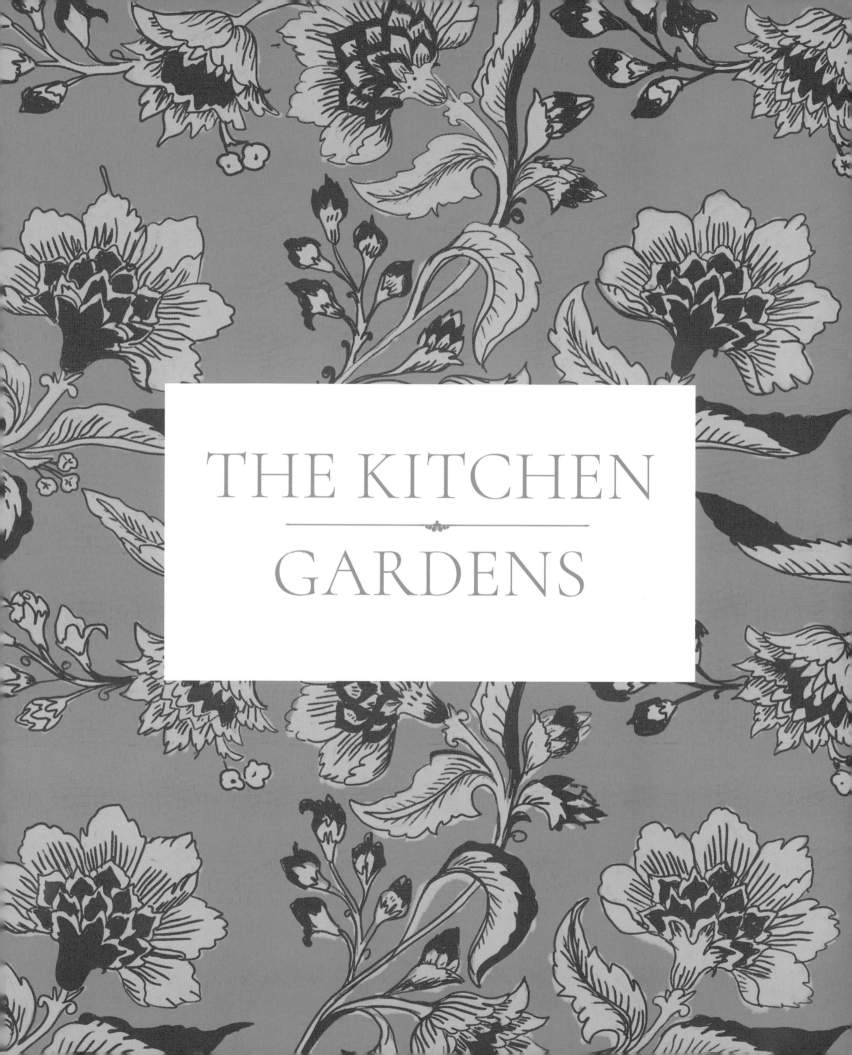

THE KITCHEN

GARDENS

EMMA BRIDGEWATER & MATTHEW RICE

Oxfordshire

Kitchen gardens have been in and out of fashion more times than turnips and cabbage. In the 1980s, the venerated garden designer Rosemary Verey prompted many gardeners to pull out their roses and plant peas and beans when she introduced the world to her now-famous potager garden at Barnsley House. The Château de Villandry in France piqued people's interest when they began to discover its ornamental parterres of purple cabbages and fall pumpkins. Then Raymond Blanc created an incredible edible garden at his Michelin-starred restaurant Le Manoir aux Quat'Saisons in Oxfordshire. For a while kitchen gardens faded from view, overtaken by formal green gardens and other styles. When former First Lady Michelle Obama put the focus firmly on vegetable gardens through her work at the White House garden (inspired by pioneers like Alice Waters) they returned to favor.

Now, thankfully, vegetable gardens are "in" again, mostly because people love the idea of fresh produce outside their front door, and Emma Bridgewater is one of them.

Bridgewater and her husband, Matthew Rice, who is a painter, designer, best-selling author of architecture books, and a founding partner of David (Viscount) Linley's furniture brand, live on a glorious Oxfordshire estate called Ham Court, which includes a spectacular kitchen garden. The story of how this garden came to be is as intriguing as the history of the castle that sits behind it.

Ham Court is made up of several buildings; the main one is a baronial-style residence. This was created out of the remains of Bampton Castle, which, during its heyday in the fourteenth

century, dominated the landscape. During the 1700s, most of the castle was demolished, but this section, once the gatehouse that formed part of the original castle wall and gate passage, survived. Much of the medieval architecture is still intact, including the vaulted ceilings, fireplaces, moulded columns, flagstone floors, arched doorways, and an octagonal stair turret with a parapet.

According to the agent who sold Ham Court to the couple, its last update was in the nineteenth century. (The stone staircases had not been touched for seven hundred years.) Bridgewater and Rice have chosen to live in one of the stone barns on the farm while the main residence is restored. (Hence, the name Bampton Castle Farm.) However, they are so content in the now-converted and surprisingly comfortable barn that they don't mind waiting for the restoration work. Another converted barn contains offices for both Bridgewater and Rice and a capacious space filled with books, ceramics, and unpainted crockery and plates, ready for visitors to unleash their creative talents in popular workshops.

It's a long way from the designer's early days in the mid-1980s, when she began making plates, mugs, jugs, and platters from a rented flat in London as she was unable find anything that appealed to her. Seeking a location for production, she found a factory in Stoke-on-Trent, famous for the Staffordshire pottery industry, and started her own line. Her business grew, from mug to mug, collection to collection. The factory now produces twenty-five thousand pieces a month, sold worldwide. Bridgewater designs often pop up on Instagram, usually as pretty teacups with posies of summer roses and tea treats.

So how does the huge kitchen garden come into the picture? Bridgewater and Rice were attracted to the property because of the derelict walled garden, which offered as much potential as the old buildings and acres of space. After they moved in, Rice became determined to revive the garden that had been there, underneath the mess of farm buildings, mud, and rubble. The vision took five years and a great deal of new topsoil to achieve. They dug a moat, planted thousands of trees, and got to work.

This kitchen garden looks like it has always been an integral part of the castle and its day-to-day routine. That is its beauty. Bridgewater and Rice have achieved the ultimate gardener's goal of making a garden feel established when it is new.

Opposite and this page: The garden at first light.

Eventually, the new garden became established, and the produce began to flourish, no doubt helped by the fertilizer of the farm animals. Now plants grow so big in summer and autumn that they submerge visitors who wander through. The gourd tunnel is a highlight, as are the greenhouses. There is now a full-time gardener, Arthur Parkinson, who also manages the factory garden.

This garden is more than just decorative. It's also used to feed Bridgewater's staff every day, as well as guests and visitors to the estate. The garden has also inadvertently inspired the couple in their business. Many of the scenes of their new country life began to appear in pastoral motifs on the company's

dinnerware, bowls, and mugs. There is even a collection called A Year in the Country. The top-selling Hen & Toast collection has become nearly as popular as the signature Toast & Marmalade.

Perhaps the real success of the castle's garden is that it looks as though it has always been there, an integral part of the landscape of the estate and the day-to-day routine. The garden feels established, even though it is very new.

It remains to be seen what happens from here, and how much more the garden can grow. But if the success of Bridgewater's pastoral-inspired pottery is anything to go by, this garden will be cultivated—and loved—for a long time.

Opposite: The gourd tunnel is also a shelter for beans.
This page: The chickens, vegetables, and birds
are inspiration for Bridgewater's pottery designs.

Top, left: Cooking in the kitchen. Top, right: Mugs by Bridgewater show the influence of the garden and country life. Above: Onions drying on a rack. Right: Vintage books offer inspiration for design ideas. Opposite: Vegetables grow as large as bushes in the fertile soil. Following spread: The castle in the early light.

JEFFREY BILHUBER

Locust Valley

Jeffrey Bilhuber is a master of color. He may be best known for his beautiful manners and style, so reminiscent of Old Hollywood stars, but his real appeal is his deft handling of unusual hues many others would hesitate to use. Few other designers come close to his painterly talents in interior palettes. Think radish red, blood orange, and pomegranate, combined with lettuce-leaf green. Walking into his wonderful weekend home, Hay Fever (named by the previous owner after the Noël Coward play), on the North Shore of Long Island, offers a study in color, and an education in style. Rooms are luminous, with walls that shimmer with drama and sophistication. The building may have once been a boys' boarding school but it's now reminiscent of a grand museum of beauty and design, only one where a steady stream of wines, whisky sours, and Aperol spritzes are freely served, laughter is abundant, and guests are allowed to recline.

Take the family dining room, which is decorated, rather deliciously, in raspberry, caramel, and rich chocolate—like a dessert of *chocolate crémeux*. Also on the ground floor, there is an enormous eighteenth-century sitting room overlooking the garden, a paean to prettiness, with a spring-green theme running through it, like shelled new spring peas. (The color is Benjamin Moore's Chic Lime). The raspberry-striped slipcovers (Candy Stripe from Sonia's Place) make the space even more uplifting.

At the end of the house, tucked away in its own wing, there is an enormous master bedroom, which resembles a luxurious hotel suite. The space is a dramatic ode to the color rouge; done in deep, plush, beautifully patterned damask. There are also persimmon lamps and a wicker stool as a surprise factor—something Bilhuber does best. It is as cozy in summer, when the doors to the patio are opened wide to allow the breeze in, as it is in winter, when the fire is lit.

Above and opposite: Hidden behind interior designer Jeffrey Bilhuber's Long Island home, a former boys' boarding school in verdant Locust Valley, the garden offers a bucolic pocket of charm to offset the grandeur of the historic residence. Once mostly vegetables, it now includes flowers and formal elements.

But it's the entrance that is the most sublime space in this country estate, with delicate turquoise-blue walls the color of Araucana eggs, a huge tufted sofa in crushed grape, like a big glass of Pinot Noir, and a hall wallpapered in a Quadrille print called Climbing Hydrangeas—a color reminiscent of Old Florida pink.

Hay Fever's interiors are fabulous, flamboyant, and so beautiful they could be the set of a Broadway show, but they are instantly welcoming and hospitable, too. Even the powder room is taxicab yellow—immediately enticing and incredibly witty. It is next to the collection of taxicab guest umbrellas resting in a chic cluster by the back door.

Where does this great love of color come from? This dedication to bold hues? Much of the interior actually takes inspiration from his colorful garden. Like many designers, Bilhuber is passionate about plants, flowers, and foliage. But he goes one step further than most in interpreting and adopting nature's fertile hues by bringing them inside, to show their glorious shades in equally glorious rooms. His country garden was for a time dominated by a charming potager, and the pigments of the fresh produce he grew—lettuces, silver beets, tomatoes, radishes, beans, and peas—were celebrated in his interior palettes. Then, when the garden was converted to a more formal design based on Edith Wharton's home, The Mount, in Lenox, Massachusetts, obelisks used for the climbing French beans were changed to elegantly shaped ivy pyramids, and different shades of green came to the fore in both his studio and his home.

But here's how Bilhuber is really clever about his design symbiosis: the garden is reflected not just in the colors of his rooms, but in myriad smaller ways. Two utterly lifelike, almost fluorescent-green, feathered sculptures on the mantel resemble

Opposite: The potager has morphed into more of a formal garden with tulips and peonies, but Bilhuber misses his produce and farmers' markets, and is considering reinstating many of the vegetable beds. Above: Wicker baskets near the outdoor shower reflect the materials of the wicker drink vessels.

the soft fronds of New Zealand tree ferns in the courtyard outside. Potted plants of climbing jasmine offer a lovely botanical pairing to a sofa upholstered in a vintage cotton printed with yellow violets and roses. And two lemon-scented geraniums in the sitting room give off the most delightful aroma as people pass and brush the leaves.

Bilhuber's skill with color is precise: he can see a pink or green and know it's too unnatural. For example, something might be too faux fuchsia. Like the great Balenciaga with his famous magentas and mauves, Bilhuber knows that choosing the right color is as much about the occasion as the light, the space, and the location (city versus country) as it is about the person living in it.

Hay Fever is a house full of love and life but it is also imbued with a gentle beauty, and much of that is a result of the garden's influence. The sweep of lawn, the pale blue pool (a color reflected in the kitchen), the grand old trees and oyster-shell driveway, the potager turned Wharton-esque garden beds, the huge Australian and New Zealand tree ferns, the dozens of Boston ferns that embroider the veranda, the clipped boxwood, and the fresh herbs for the meals served to guests all reflect the glorious relationship between nature and man, and pay tribute to a designer whose incredible talent for merging gardens and interiors makes enlivening, inspiring, and extraordinary homes.

Above: Ethereal green feathers reflect the forms of the New Zealand tree ferns and other foliage in the garden. Opposite: Jeffrey Bilhuber's clients include the late David Bowie, Iman, Mariska Hargitay, Michael Douglas, Hubert de Givenchy, and Anna Wintour. His work has a high glamour quotient. But he also designs for comfort, kids, and pets. Rooms are made to be lived in.

Left: The house, called Hay Fever (named after the Noël Coward play), was built in 1668, but has been modernized over the past 350 years without losing its grace or grandeur. Above: Gardens, like the weather, are ever-changing, and this one has morphed from a kitchen to a partial formal garden, inspired by Edith Wharton's garden at The Mount, to one having a mixture of everything, including tulips and peonies. The green, pink, purple, and red palette is reflected in the dramatic rooms inside.

Opposite: Bilhuber is a master of color. His interiors often use combinations that few other designers would consider. Many of his ideas for these unusual medleys come from the colors in nature, gardens, and in particular his beloved former vegetable garden. The lettuce-green and tomato-red sitting room is an extension of the potager that was located at the rear of the house, near the kitchen, and was filled with colorful produce in the summer months. Above: Bilhuber working in his potager, before it morphed to a more formal garden, with flower beds.

Bilhuber consulted with the curators at Monticello and Mount Vernon to determine historically accurate paint colors for some of his house's interiors. The overall design, however, is a tribute to his talent and creativity. The egg-yolk-yellow hall and bathroom are as inviting as breakfast on a sunny weekend; there is a hall wallpapered in the color of ripe watermelons; a pale turquoise-and-plum sitting room that works fantastically well, and a main bedroom that is a display of pageantry in red and a glamorous Old Hollywood beige. It's a flamboyant, wildly imaginative home, and yet it's instantly warm and hospitable, too.

A table set for luncheon on one of the two verandas. The colors reflect the hues of the garden in spring, with its pink peonies and crimson tulips.

ROBIN STANDEFER & STEPHEN ALESCH
(ROMAN AND WILLIAMS)

Montauk

Montauk is not an ideal place for gardeners. The ocean winds that blow off the end of Long Island can be determinedly destructive. The salinity can be merciless, the soil sandy. Many give up and head inland. Montauk gardens need to be tough. And, Montauk gardeners need to be resilient and resourceful.

Nobody knows this better than Montauk residents Robin Standefer and Stephen Alesch. They are founders of one of New York's leading architectural and interior design firms Roman and Williams, which has become internationally famous for projects, including the celebrated Le Coucou restaurant, The Ace and The Standard Hotels, the lobby of The Royalton Hotel, and many other design destinations across the United States.

Standefer started her career as a production and set designer in Hollywood, working with directors such as Martin Scorsese and conceptualizing the look of movies including *Zoolander* and *Practical Magic*. She and Alesch, a former art director who trained as an architect, gradually moved to residential projects after actors such as Ben Stiller asked them to do houses that had the atmosphere of their film sets. (The couple has since designed spaces for Gwyneth Paltrow and Kate Hudson.)

The core of their work is narrative; telling a great story—or back story—about a place, but with architecture and objects. People go to Roman and Williams's commercial spaces to see the design and the collections that speak of nostalgia as much as they do to partake in the social scene. The couple's other skill is creating

Opposite: Robin Standefer and Stephen Alesch's garden feels like a secret hideaway by the ocean.
Above: Standefer on a swing in a corner of the garden.

places that feel timeless rather than contrived; places that feel rooted in their surroundings with a conviction that's apparent to all those who enter them. The couple loves to source architectural elements for buildings. Consequently the spaces they design feel familiar, even though they may have just been restored or rebuilt. They are masters of making the new look comfortably old, and the old look cool again.

When it came to their own residential escape, it made sense that they went looking for something they could restore, and they found it in the low-key fishing-surfing village of Montauk. Alesch is a surfer and Standefer a gardener, and they could pursue both passions there. Montauk is also a long way, geographically, architecturally, and spiritually, from Manhattan's urban madness, which was a change they welcomed.

Serendipitously they stumbled upon a modest, two-bedroom 1970s "contractor special" tossed together with a nail gun and some discounted plywood. It was ripe for the Roman and Williams treatment. They took their time with the renovations,

wanting to be sure they were creating a home that was comfortable while still retaining the authenticity and old-fashioned charm of the 1970s design.

Slowly, Montauk became their retreat from the world but it also became their second design studio, a place where concepts were born over a beer and a barbecue on a summer night, after a day spent in the surf. The duo found there was aesthetic stimulation everywhere they looked, and many of the house's architectural elements were used elsewhere, in their commercial projects. The exposed ceilings inspired them to do a similar look for Facebook's mess hall; the tambour walls were replicated for The Royalton and The Standard Hotels.

Soon Montauk became a place fostering creativity as much as serenity. Of imagination as much as relaxation. It also became a house that celebrated the handmade, the heartfelt, things that had integrity, and soul. Almost everything in the beach house has an interesting provenance. Things that haven't been handmade have been collected from much-loved destinations. Or salvaged from somewhere.

Above: Sunflowers growing in the new garden, a plot of land bought recently to extend the original garden. Opposite: The interior of the beach house is a mix of architectural and design flotsam and jetsam: pieces found during travels, much-loved artwork, and uniquely designed furniture.

The philosophy of appreciating simplicity extended to the garden. Standefer has long adored gardens—her movie garden and conservatory in the Nicole Kidman/Sandra Bullock film *Practical Magic* was such a hit people still post images of it on Pinterest and blogs. Alesch also appreciates gardens, and they both admire the work of British landscape architects Capability Brown and Gertrude Jekyll. Capability Brown's designs for mostly estate and palace gardens were more formal and manicured than Jekyll's, whose designs tended to be wild. The couple appreciates both styles, and wanted to create a mixture of the two. "We wanted something that had a well-planned, orderly feel but we also wanted something with an almost fairy-tale look, and the sense that the plants had been growing there for many years," says Standefer.

They relished this chance to create a hideaway by the ocean, a small but intimate garden that was able to withstand the harsh environment while still nurturing plants—and nurturing themselves, too. "We go to Montauk every weekend, year-round, and it's a complete escape for us, as well as being a design laboratory. In spring and summer, starting in March, we garden every day that we're there. Gardening gives you a humbling insight into control: you give so much love to a plant but you can't control the weather changes. It's been a good lesson for us to learn—both in the garden and in life."

"Gardens by the ocean are particularly challenging," continues Standefer. "We have certainly struggled with ours at times. We love flowers and roses, but certain things aren't hardy enough for the Montauk environment. The harsh seasons and dramatic weather meant that we had to learn to choose hardy plants that could survive in this type of formidable climate. This struggle to find the right plants for this environment is what really started our love of the culinary garden—as well as the fact that our gardening became connected to our food and cooking."

The garden wraps right around the beach house, but it is the potager, with its vegetables and herbs, that is closest to their hearts. Tethered at one end with a double arbor and enclosed by a simple timber fence, it has the feel of the magical Madoo Conservancy garden in Sagaponack—although the couple also cites medieval potagers in France as inspiration, as well as the Jardin des Plantes in Paris.

"That whole tradition of mixing flowers and vegetables in an artful way is fundamental to our entire garden," says Standefer. Like the house, the garden has a rusticity about it—sapling obelisks; beds etched in beach pebbles; deckchairs set on the lawn for après-garden Aperols. It perfectly suits the house's interior, with its raw, unpainted, exposed beams, white timber walls, and painted stairs.

The planting scheme is mostly herbs and vegetables—heirloom tomatoes are a favorite—and includes lettuces, radishes, peppers, pumpkins, eggplant, artichokes, and chervil, as well as more exotic options from around the world, like cardoons. "We love using the garden to expose ourselves to herbs and plants from different parts of the world. This past summer we grew cardoons from Italy and shiso from Japan, and we also grew these giant scallions that were from Japanese seeds, which were just fantastic. Growing seeds and plants from different parts of the world is something that captivates us. We are doing a project in Amsterdam right now, and we bought this unusual Dutch cabbage called rosenkohl that's just been amazing. The garden has added to our love of travel—sometimes we grow the plant before we go to the place!"

In summer months, the kitchen garden is so healthy that the pair often asks their restaurant clients in Manhattan if they'd like some of the overflow of produce. They've become so passionate about their potager that they purchased another

The garden is a mix of formality and rusticity. It is primarily a vegetable garden, although in the spirit of the traditional potager it has flowers as well. During summer, the produce is abundant enough for the couple to offer surplus to their restaurant clients.

acre in 2016, where they planted corn and sunflowers. "We call this new land 'the farm,'" says Standefer. "I tend the kitchen garden and Stephen tends the farm." Alesch has already started experimenting with crops, including forcing radicchio. "There's a poetry to this," he says. "Winter comes and you take a plant that looks completely dead and put it in a man-made stream. After a while, you peel these dead leaves away and you find the most beautiful, vibrant little vegetable. In the dead of winter, it's such a metamorphosis." In addition to the farm, they've made plans to put in a little orchard—"we'll start with four apple trees to begin with."

The success of the coastal garden, in this wild, windswept place, has inspired them to add garden design to their business, although "sometimes it's not economically feasible," says Standefer.

"We always suggest it to our clients, but it depends on climate and site. We did a project on Nantucket [Greydon House] and collaborated with the landscape designer Marty McGowan of Sconset Gardener, who also owns this beautiful organic farm called Pumpkin Pond. And he created these amazing flower boxes and a small garden for a hotel we designed. We had such a strong connection with him, and he liked the idea of mixing vegetables, herbs, and flowers. It was the foundation for our overall inspiration for that project."

The couple also designed a garden for Le Coucou restaurant in New York City. "The owner really embraced the idea of putting in a garden right on the street. The restaurant feels a bit like a French country house in the middle of Manhattan, and the idea was that it would be a beautiful respite. Since we created that garden, there are these lovely fuzzy fat sparrows that nest in the trees that we planted, which is really gratifying."

What they love most, however, is returning to their own garden, in a hidden corner of Montauk, a few surfboards from the ocean. "Stephen and I have always had tremendous interest, since childhood, in plants and nature, and that was a great bond for us in our relationship. From structure and scents to color, the natural world has been our greatest inspiration. It's always fascinated and captivated us, and now it's become our obsession!"

Above: The garden produces prodigious quantities of radishes, peppers, pumpkins, eggplant, artichokes, and chervil, as well as more exotic options from around the world, such as cardoons.

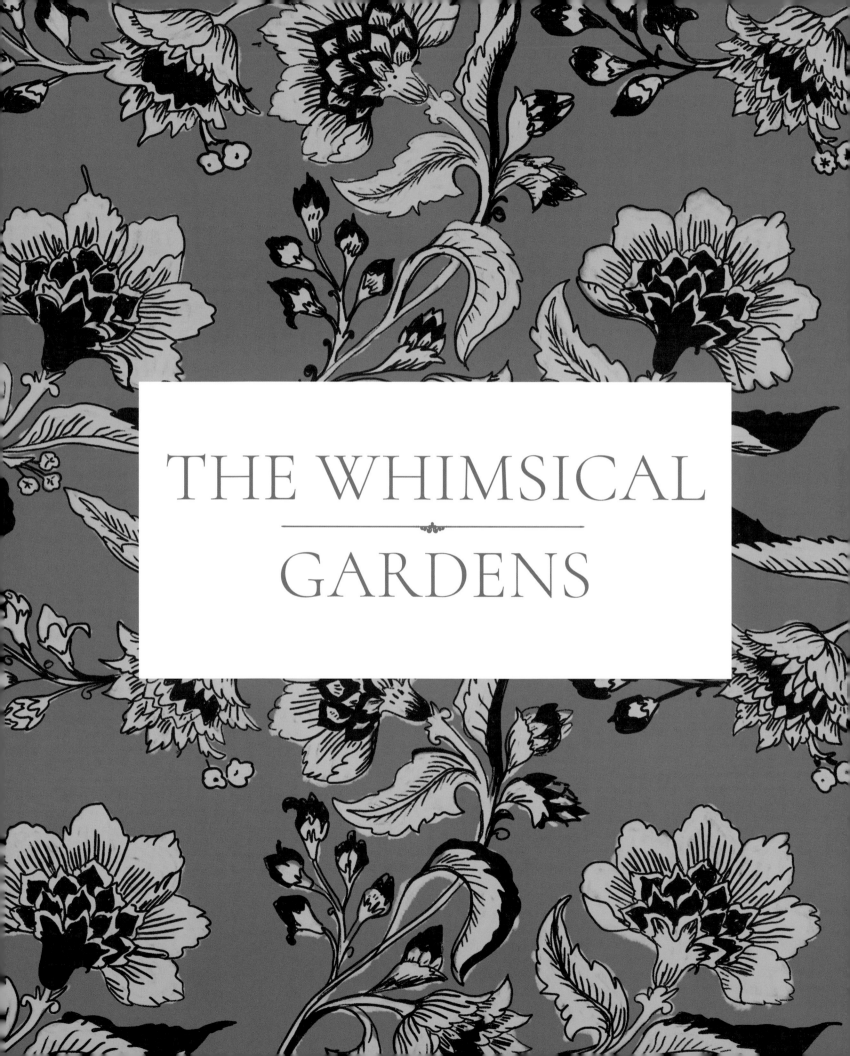

THE WHIMSICAL
GARDENS

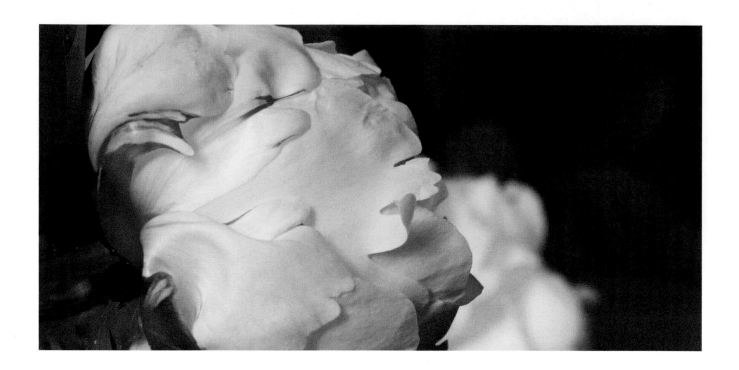

BARNABA FORNASETTI

Milan

When Italian designer Pietro Fornasetti built his grand, four-story Milan home in the late nineteenth century, the surrounding area was mostly fruit and vegetable fields. The verdant green space with its views and acres of tranquility was the perfect landscape to inspire his son Piero Fornasetti, whose imaginative designs became world famous. In the ensuing years, however, the landscape dramatically changed. Now called Città Studi, this busy residential part of the city is full of mopeds driven by students of the nearby polytechnic university. But the villa and garden, which has been home to Pietro Fornasetti, his son, Piero Fornasetti, and now his son, Barnaba Fornasetti, is still much the same. The garden is a bucolic, country-style sanctuary in the middle of Milan's fast-moving metropolis. And the house, with its many wings and its old rooms echoing with history and curiosities, is a time warp of the most delightful treasures. There is character in every corner, creaky floorboard, and crevice. And while the plan has changed over time, as rooms have been added and moved, it has remained a family home, albeit one that looks like a museum. A museum of Fornasetti magnificence.

Piero Fornasetti, son of Pietro, was an Italian painter, sculptor, printmaker, interior decorator, and prolific designer whose talents came to light when he started producing extraordinary objects with graphic imagery based on Roman ruins, suns, and flowers. Fornasetti's iconography was original and inventive

Above and opposite: Italian designer Barnaba Fornasetti's secret garden in the heart of Milan is a fantastical, wonderful oasis; a rambling plan of hydrangeas, roses, peonies, rustic tools, and welcoming seats that look as enticing from leaf level as from above. It's little wonder that its textures, colors, and patterns constantly show up in Fornasetti's designs. Like the house, the garden feels very lived-in; there is a charming sense of imperfection to it. "I like it a little wild," says Fornasetti, who finds it a pleasing contrast to the stresses and pressures of modern-day life.

Top, left: A great deal of Barnaba Fornasetti's time is spent delving through his father's extensive archive of fine drawings in order to create new prints in a process that he calls "reinvention and re-edition." Top, right, and opposite: The garden shows up in Fornasetti's collections in curious ways. This popular design of keys hanging in a privet hedge, called *Chiavi Segrete*, has become a best seller. Above: A Fornasetti chest stands in front of a green-shelved library of books and architectural prints.

while paying respect to the classics—including neoclassical architecture, botany, and books. Fornasetti would twist these familiar images so they were recognizable but still curiously romantic, and then put them on everything from dinner plates to multi-paneled screens, bureaus, umbrella stands, small trays, and silk scarves. There were also collections of more wondrous designs, with images of opera singers, after he became obsessed with Lina Cavalieri, the Italian early twentieth-century soprano and actress. Fornasetti's career saw him create more than thirteen thousand pieces, an incredible career feat.

Piero's son Barnaba is now the head of the family design firm, and, like his father, has an incredible gift for design. He often utilizes his father's ideas to create new designs, with the result that classic and contemporary motifs often merge in fantastical collections.

The Fornasetti house is filled to the rafters with Fornasetti designs, from decorative pieces to entire rooms. As Barnaba says, "It's a house, a workshop and office, an archive, an atelier, and a museum, too."

The key to Barnaba's success is his art of storytelling. A great raconteur, he may seem shy, but with a little encouragement he offered to show me around the garden and told the story of his first design idea, when he was three. "I picked a hydrangea and my father used it as a motif on a tray."

The garden and its botanical motifs continue to inspire him, decades on. A recent design called Ortensia was drawn from the mauve-blue hydrangeas that surround the house in summer. Designs of leaves, keys, flowers, and clouds have each been used on wallpaper, in candles, and on china and furniture.

Opposite: A corner of the Fornasetti family home reveals some of the treasures that lie within the residence, including a stunning folding screen covered in a vintage travel map print, called *Battaglia Navale/Libri*, now a collector's piece. Above: A recent Fornasetti design called Ortensia was inspired by the huge bank of mauve-blue hydrangeas that surround the house in summer.

Above: A vintage Fornasetti design for an umbrella stand, now
a collector's piece. Opposite: The garden that inspired it.

The garden also makes its presence felt in the house itself, particularly in the white, conservatory-style kitchen where butterflies have been printed onto almost every surface to create a dazzling display of Lepidoptera. When the doors are opened and butterflies drift inside, it becomes a glorious example of the designs of man meeting Mother Nature.

Elsewhere in the garden, there are blousy bunches of peonies, charming wrought-iron chairs, paths that amble this way and that, a secret potting shed in the corner, and roses dotted here and there. (Both the peonies and the garden's foliage have shown up in Fornasetti prints.) It has the feel of a country garden, a romantic relic of when the residence was surrounded by fruit and vegetable orchards. Piero and Barnaba have drawn on that pastoral history for many of their designs, particularly *Cesto*

di frutta ("fruit basket"), which was designed by Piero in the 1950s and is still part of the design repertoire. A lithograph of it printed on lacquered multilayered wood and hand-painted hangs in the kitchen, where it replaced a painting of a butterfly seller, *La Venditrice di farfalle*. The painting was included in the exhibition Piero Fornasetti: 100 Years of Practical Madness at Milan's Triennale Design Museum in the winter of 2013-2014.

The most famous of the Fornasetti images is the iconic beauty Lina Cavalieri; collectors also buy the more imaginary prints of library shelves laden with old books. But perhaps the favorite for gardeners looking for a piece of Fornasetti magic is Chiavi Segrete, which depicts mysterious keys hanging within a dense privet hedge. It feels like the garden that inspired it; a little wild, a little overgrown, and full of surprises.

This page and opposite: The kitchen is dominated by a large reproduction Murano chandelier, which hangs above a round table covered in a print depicting butterflies, called *Ultime Notizie* and designed by Barnaba Fornasetti. It was inspired by both a painting called *La venditrice di farfalle* (*The Butterfly Seller*), and the butterflies that float into the kitchen from the garden outside. Following spread: The iconic design *Nuvole*, which depicts a cloudy sky, in a bedroom of the villa.

CELERIE KEMBLE

Dominican Republic

Celerie Kemble is a fan of the color pink. She was an enthusiast long before it became fashionable and known as "Millennial Pink." She finds it uplifting. But it has to be the right shade—the delicate, feminine pink found in shells, or summer peonies, or Palm Beach. These are Kemble pinks. So it's no surprise to see, upon arriving at the sublime estate of Playa Grande in the Dominican Republic, that pale pink rules the interior design, along with sky blue and a palette of sympathetic pastels in between. This place has style in spades. It is also no surprise that when Playa Grande opened in 2015, it was one of the most Instagrammed places in the world.

The New York–based Kemble usually works in the United States (her company Kemble Interiors has offices in New York, Palm Beach, and London), but an opportunity to do something in the Dominican Republic was too good to pass up. The property

started life in 2014 as a getaway for Kemble and her family, their children, and friends. The two-thousand-acre site on an idyllic beach on the north shore of the island was such a beautiful landscape, between the jungle and the ocean, that the idea was floated to create more than one beach house; a collection, like an old-fashioned summer camp, but a sophisticated one. The Playa Grande Beach Club was developed, and many influential shareholders joined the party. Today, Playa Grande still feels like a family hideaway, but now the enclave of beach cottages can accommodate a crowd.

Playa Grande is Kemble's most remarkable, and certainly her most memorable, design project. She says it was "a dream" to work on, and it shows. Hidden from the world, the estate has a sense of mystery and dreaminess about it. Entering this enclave is similar to stumbling upon a curious Wes Anderson film

Above and opposite: The club house and library at Playa Grande sit in a lush garden filled with *Dypsis Lutescens* (areca palms), *Cananga Odorata* (ylang-ylang), *Terminala Catappa* (almond trees), and *Crescentia Cujete* (calabash trees).

set, only in the Caribbean instead of Budapest. The colonial Caribbean-style architecture (a combination of French, British, and Dominican) reflects the spirit of the region. Its medley of whirls and twirls have a fairy-tale-like quality. The larger bungalows display Dominican details such as *tragaluz* (transoms) in patterned woodwork over the doors. Throughout the property are ornate, doubled-pitched green tin roofs, gingerbread fretwork, louvered doors and fanlights, romantic, wraparound verandas, perfect lawns, and acres of lacelike trellis.

Inside, the beach houses have equally wondrous elements. Each is a mix of flea-market finds, antiques, and custom-made pieces. Fabrics are cheerful and include Muriel Brandolini floral cottons. It's cluttered but deliberately so. The feeling is one of comfort; you can drag sand into these beach bungalows without worry. The outdoor furniture, a mix of vintage wicker and rattan pieces, also fits in. (Kemble collects garden elements and says elegant old wicker is "coming back" into garden fashion. In fact, she recently designed a wallpaper for Schumacher called Wicker Stripe.)

Opposite and above: The clubhouse at Playa Grande features foliage-shaped lights inspired by the garden, playful pieces found at flea markets and auctions, and wicker furniture, which is making a comeback.

Ceilings and floors are painted in pastel shades to complement the rest of the architecture—the clubhouse's twenty-two-foot-high ceilings are pale aqua—while the handmade tiles are pink, yellow, and blue. (Shell pink and pale aqua-blue are dominant shades.) The kitchens are deliberately retro in style, while the bathrooms are one-part preppy chic and one-part beach-house boho. Everything has a charm that harks back to the halcyon days of childhood vacations.

To create this enchanting hideaway, Kemble worked with builder Marc Johnson and historic preservationist Elric Endersby. She also commissioned local craftsmen, including Pedro Noesi of Dominican design studio Neno Industrial, to make the copper lanterns and light fittings. These have a verdigris patina so that

when they age they will blend in with the garden. Design-wise, it is perhaps these pieces that set this place apart. Everywhere you look, these foliage-inspired lights dot the estate. There are lanterns shaped like palm trees, lights like lily of the valley bouquets, and even four-poster beds with copper ivy leaves "growing" up the sides. It's exquisite—a tropical wonderland where nature seems to have taken over.

The rest of the furnishings, materials, and decorative elements were selected to be just as sensitive to the surroundings. There are honey-colored cane pieces, sea grass mats, grayed teak, weathered zinc fixtures, and painted and worn wicker seating. Everything is designed to be comfortable, sturdy, and child friendly, but also very chic.

This page and opposite: The effect the garden at Playa Grande has had on the architecture and interior is evident in every corner of the estate, particularly in the designs of the lights and lanterns. Following spread: The exterior of the library.

The beach houses on the estate are slightly different, but the one thing they all have in common is the theme of gardens. Each features botanical prints, lights sculptured like foliage, and beds carved out of copper ivy, as well as spaces that flow from interior to garden in a seamless style.

As for the garden, the planting scheme looks at ease in the natural landscape as does the architecture. Palm trees soar into the blue Dominican sky; thickets of lush foliage create privacy around beach houses; and small stone paths wind gently from building to building, then onto the clubhouse and nearby dining room. It feels natural, even though it's been carefully thought out and landscaped to accommodate people.

Kemble and her architects, designers, and gardeners, Juan Diego Garcia and Whandy Martinez, have made a point of trying to preserve the vegetation. (The road to reach Playa Grande is lined with palm plantations.) It is a sympathetic planting scheme of native trees and flowering plants, which both adds to the tropical growth and maximizes privacy for those seeking it. Against a backdrop of bold green foliage, there are many colorful flowers, including orchids, jacarandas, frangipani trees, jasmine, hibiscus, ginger, and many kinds of heliconias. The trees and green foliage plants include coconut palms, Dypsis Lutescens (areca palms), Cananga Odorata (ylang-ylang), Terminala Catappa (almond trees), Crescentia Cujete (calabash trees), and Bursera simaruba, commonly known as gumbo-limbo, copperwood, chaca, or turpentine tree.

Playa Grande isn't a hotel. Nor is it a private home. It's a quiet, curious, sublimely stylish retreat that falls somewhere in between the two—a hideaway that fuses garden, island, and architecture in one effortless, elegant package.

Opposite and above: The garden is designed to be a lush landscape of palms and plants, ranging from orchids and jacarandas to almond trees and even ylang-ylang. Following spread: The designs of the lights were inspired by the forms of the garden. Kemble hired a local craftsman, Pedro Noesi of Dominican design studio Neno Industrial, to create the copper lanterns, light fittings, and botanical-inspired beds. These have a verdigris patina so when they age they will look like the rest of the lush green plants and palms on the estate.

Above, top: A garden swing attached to a charming arbor provides a place to sit and read. Above: A rattan light in the pool house evokes the texture of a coconut husk. Right: The pool and beach are edged in coconut palms and tropical almond trees.

Acknowledgments

Just as many gardens do, this book took on a life of its own and engaged more and more of us as it evolved through the years and seasons. It grew from being a one-person project to a grand opera of international gardens and their owners, gardeners, staff, assistants, publicists, and many others along the way who helped facilitate the often-complex photography shoots.

This book was actually a happy accident. In 2014 I had pitched the concept for a publication on private libraries of architects and designers, but my Rizzoli editor wasn't convinced. "What other ideas do you have?" she asked kindly. "Well," I began tentatively, "I have an idea for a garden book, but I'm not sure it's commercially viable, either." To my surprise, however, the Rizzoli team adored the proposal, and so began three years of memorable photo shoots all over the world, photographing some of the most magnificent gardens and homes I've ever had the good fortune to be invited into.

There was a shoot at the Provence garden of the late Nicole de Vésian, the former director of the lifestyle collections of Hermès, which took four flights and twenty-four hours to reach from Australia, via Asia, but worth all the air miles when I wandered through her "horticultural tapestry" during that beautiful blue hour at twilight, tearful with the beauty of it all.

There was a shoot at Playa Grande in the Dominican Republic, just before a major hurricane hit. (I was the only guest left in the hotel; it felt like a "horticultural" version of *The Shining*.) The estate and its garden—a six-hour round-trip from my hotel—was so remote that not even the driver—a veteran guide of the Dominican Republic—knew it was there. He was just as enchanted by Playa Grande as I was. Driving back to the hotel through tiny villages and stunning coastal scenery, the driver told me stories of the island, his family and his descendants, and his love for this extraordinary country. I flew in and out of the Dominican Republic in three days, and I would not have missed it for all the hurricanes in the world.

And there was the sublime triptych of English garden shoots that began with a day at Ben Pentreath and Charlie McCormick's famous garden The Parsonage in Dorset, which has long been one of the stars of Instagram. It was followed by a day at Paolo Moschino and Philip Vergeylen's elegant home in West Sussex, hearing wonderful stories about gardens and travel over a beautiful luncheon and slightly potent wine. (Thankfully we'd shot most of the garden by then or it might have been a "very blurry" chapter!) It was then finished with Emma Bridgewater and Matthew Rice's grand estate in Oxfordshire, surely one of the most beautiful private potager gardens in the world. By the time Emma and Matthew's shoot came around, however, I was so weary from travel, and so terrified I'd miss Matthew's suggested start time of 6:00 a.m., that I drove to their farm at 4:30 a.m. and waited outside, watching an exquisite English sunrise unfurl like a huge orange dahlia over the horizon. It was one of those moments that makes life worthwhile.

Like the photographer Horst P. Horst, I don't believe in manipulating spaces to create better photographs. The idea of bringing a truckload of props to someone's home, and then spending days with a huge team re-arranging their treasured furniture in their cherished rooms seems wrong to me—and, increasingly, many others in this business. The idea is to capture people as they live at home, not in a staged set, and the thought of moving even a bed or a table seems inappropriate and disrespectful. Gloria Vanderbilt once said that Horst didn't move a single chair or bring in extra flowers, that he showed how people really lived, and I think that's what so many of us want to see now: homes with character, personality, and authenticity. That is why publications like *Cabana* and *The World of Interiors* are so successful. And so this book shows designers just as they are, with their messy book piles, and their Wellington boots, and their dogs, and their paperwork. These are all spectacular homes but they are also much-loved spaces where their owners retreat at the end of a busy work week, to pour a drink and put up their feet.

As I said, this book was an ambitious undertaking that took several years and many people on several continents to make happen. I would like to sincerely thank the people on the following pages for their time, patience, and graciousness. It was largely due to the kindness of these designers and their efficient teams that we managed to achieve this wonderful publication. Thank you for opening your homes and gardens, and for all the lovely luncheons on the lawns and terraces, and for the stories and laughter that followed. (Jeffrey Bilhuber, Paolo Moschino, and Philip Vergeylen: I will never forget your wonderful tales.)

I would like to extend a special thank you to those designers and photographers who kindly contributed images when we were unable to shoot gardens, or parts of gardens, due to time constraints or inclement weather. Thank you to the House of Dior, the Christian Dior Museum, and Dior's photographers. Thank you to Carolyne Roehm, Stephen Alesch, Mikkel Vang, Ariadna Bufi, Jeffrey Bilhuber, and Bill Richards.

Last but not least, I would like to sincerely thank Charles Miers and Sandy Gilbert Freidus of Rizzoli New York for commissioning this idea, my book designers Alissa Dinallo and Lisa Dyke for designing it under my art direction, and my friend, the best-selling author and interior designer, Tricia Foley, for helping to persuade Rizzoli that an author and photographer from Australia, so far away from New York, could produce such an ambitious book. Thank you all for supporting this beautiful project. I am deeply grateful.

—JANELLE McCULLOCH

Sincere thanks to the following designers and their teams, publicity companies, and other contacts for their kind assistance (listed in order of the chapters in this book). Most of the chapters are based on conversations I had with the designers as I photographed their gardens, in addition to my research into their histories, careers, and collections. Robin Standefer of Roman and Williams was especially kind enough to respond at length to my Q&A interview in January 2017.

DAVID HICKS, OXFORDSHIRE: Lady Pamela Hicks, Ashley Hicks, Paul Ballard.

ROBERT COUTURIER, CONNECTICUT: Robert Couturier, Jeffrey Morgan, Clive Lodge, Joseph Ramirez, Katharina Plath.

NICOLE DE VÉSIAN / LA LOUVE, PROVENCE: Monsieur and Madame Pascale, Sylvie Verger-Lanel, Louisa Jones.

PAOLO MOSCHINO, WEST SUSSEX: Paolo Moschino, Philip Vergeylen, Toni French Turner, Alexandra Lima.

CHRISTIAN DIOR, NORMANDY: Paule Gilles, Jerome Gautier, Perrine Scherrer, Philippe le Moult, Raphaël Dautigny, Virginie Frouin, Brigitte Richart, Lazi Hamani.

CAROLYNE ROEHM, CONNECTICUT: Carolyne Roehm, Rosa Costa, Georgia Lewis, and Carolyne's staff and gardeners, including Antonio Oliveira, Maria de Oliveira, Casey Flanagan, Carol Winters.

BUNNY WILLIAMS, CONNECTICUT: Bunny Williams, John Rosselli, Carolyn Coulter, and Bunny's staff and gardeners.

AERIN LAUDER, HAMPTONS: Aerin Lauder, Teresa Sartorius, Jacqueline Menda, Dorina Hawkins, Tina Cooke.

BEN PENTREATH, DORSET: Ben Pentreath, Charlie McCormick, Zoe Wightman.

GARY McBOURNIE, NANTUCKET: Gary McBournie, Bill Richards, Julie Wood.

EMMA BRIDGEWATER, OXFORDSHIRE: Emma Bridgewater, Matthew Rice, Arthur Parkinson, Sarah Davis.

JEFFREY BILHUBER, LOCUST VALLEY: Jeffrey Bilhuber, Levi Blasdel.

ROBIN STANDEFER AND STEPHEN ALESCH (ROMAN AND WILLIAMS), MONTAUK: Robin Standefer, Stephen Alesch, Daniella Weinberg, Marianne Boschert.

BARNABA FORNASETTI, MILAN: Barnaba Fornasetti, Yuki Tintori, Silvia Somaschini, Elisabetta Lapadula, Fabio Il Gardiniere, Robyn Lea.

CELERIE KEMBLE, DOMINICAN REPUBLIC: Celerie Kemble and her business partners, Mimi McMakin, Courtney Scioscia, the staff of Playa Grande, Juan Diego Garcia, Whandy Martinez.

PHOTOGRAPHY CREDITS

First published in the United States of America in 2018
by Rizzoli International Publications, Inc.
300 Park Avenue South
New York, NY 10010
www.rizzoliusa.com

2018 2019 2020 2021 / 10 9 8 7 6 5 4 3 2 1

Printed in China

ISBN 13: 978-0-8478-6189-7

Library of Congress Control Number: 2017956531

Project Editor: Sandra Gilbert Freidus, with assistance from Elizabeth Smith, Deborah Gardner,
Sara Pozefsky, and Tricia Levi

Art Direction: Janelle McCulloch, with assistance from Alissa Dinallo,
Lisa Dyke, and Kayleigh Jankowski

Production: Susan Lynch

Front cover: Urn in the garden of David Hicks and Lady Pamela Hicks. Back cover: Bunny Williams's
sunken garden. Page 2: Tulips in Carolyne Roehm's Connecticut garden. Page 4: Fashion and garden books
in the author's sunroom. Page 5: A sitting room in Jeffrey Bilhuber's weekend home in Locust Valley.
Page 6: A swath of scented hyacinths in Roehm's cutting garden. Page 237: Lavender baskets in Paolo
Moschino and Philip Vergeylen's West Sussex garden. Pages 238–239: The Provence garden of Nicole de Vésian.